Miracles Happen

TERRY G. PRICE

authorHOUSE®

AuthorHouse™
1663 Liberty Drive
Bloomington, IN 47403
www.authorhouse.com
Phone: 1 (800) 839-8640

Published by AuthorHouse 06/09/2017

ISBN: 978-1-5246-9659-7 (sc)
ISBN: 978-1-5246-9657-3 (hc)
ISBN: 978-1-5246-9658-0 (e)

Library of Congress Control Number: 2017910272

Print information available on the last page.

Acknowledgments

I give special thanks to my wife, Cindy, for helping me write this book. I thank Mom for praying for me when I needed it, especially before I was saved. I give thanks to my grandson, Caleb, for his influence to write this book and everyone who has had a positive influence in my life.

In memory of my brother, T.J., who died with cancer on August 20, 2013 who was a free-lance comedy script writer for radio stations. Also, my cousin's husband, Tom Clements, who died from a gunshot wound in his home on March 19, 2013, the Chief of the Colorado prisons.

I dedicate this book to my family and friends who helped to make this possible with their life experiences. I am thankful for all of their prayers for me and the miracles that they helped to bring in my life.

Most of all, I dedicate this book to the Lord Jesus Christ and I am thankful for all of the miracles He has brought me in my life.

Foreword

According to <u>The Complete Christian Dictionary for Home School and Office</u>, a *miracle* is, "An event that appears unexplainable by the laws of nature and so is held to be supernatural."

Even for evolution to take place, it requires a miracle. The first living cell required a membrane (or skin) to hold all of its elements together because without a membrane it could not possibly survive in water or all of its organs would dissolve and scatter. It would also have to replicate itself before it dies.

Evolution is so improbable that it's impossible. Only God could put it all together from nothing and make it a living organism, since it is absolutely beyond any remote chance of coming to life on its own. Only God can make the impossible to be possible. There is no real way to calculate the possibility of this spontaneous occurrence; therefore, it takes more faith to believe in evolution unaided by a Creator.

We try to explain away miracles with empirical reasoning. We use the five senses of sight, taste, hearing, smell, and touch ignoring two other senses that are important; the sense of the supernatural and common sense. The supernatural can usually be observed with instruments that accentuate the senses. When we use our brain, we are using common sense.

Common sense says if something is too improbable then it is. I try to use that kind of sense whenever I can. It seems to help me make the right decisions. I believe God gave me this sense so the Holy Spirit can work in my life to tell right from wrong. This ability to reason is a blessing that God can only give.

Miracles also include visions, daydreams, night dreams and God speaking to our hearts. These miracles always happen for God's divine will. I have heard of people having strange dreams they claim God has given them. I have learned, when they give predictions that go against the teachings of the Bible, to stay away from them because they are false prophets.

A couple good examples of these are when they start giving dates for the Rapture or if they say that the Rapture will not happen until after the Tribulation Period. A careful study of the scriptures can expose these false prophecies.

Some dialogues in this book are written to the best of my knowledge. Some names or last names have been omitted to protect the integrity of my friends.

Contents

Introduction xv

My Beginnings 1

How God Taught Me Humility 7

A New Beginning and a Changed Life 13

My Miracle Cure 16

Running Cross Country and Track 17

Praying I Could Do My Best 23

Longview Community College 27

Twin Miracles 29

Miracles at Tennessee Temple College 31

Miracles in Kansas City 36

First Lady Rosalynn Carter 39

Back to College 41

A Demonic Experience 44

A Divine Meeting 46

Learning Humility Again 47

A Classroom of Miracles 50

A Miracle Unfolding 52

A Miracle Meeting 54

A Wedding That Almost Wasn't 56

God Protected Our Honeymoon 58

Cindy's Car Miracles...60
Moving to Columbia, Missouri..63
God's Protection in the Army 64
A Tour in Hawaii...66
The Miracle That Might Have Happened.............................68
Trusting in the Lord..70
A Miracle that Didn't Happen..73
A Miracle in Jackson, Tennessee...75
Donny's Miracle 78
A Small Miracle...79
A Miracle Cure and Another 17...80
The Sign Again 81
The Psychic's Sign 82
The Eighth 17 Miracle 83
An Unexpected Miracle 85
The Wobbly Wheel 86
A Letter to a Psychic 88
Cindy and Her "Grandfather" 90
God's Revenge..91
Demons at Work..92
Bringing T.J. back to the Lord 94
Plasma Donations..95
The 360 Miracle...96

APPENDIX A: Price Genealogy in America..........................99
APPENDIX B: Love to the World (Lyrics) 101
APPENDIX C: We're So Glad You Came (Poem) 103
                Dear Christian, Good Morning (Lyrics) 103
APPENDIX D: How Much Faith Do I Need
                for Miracles to Happen?....................................105

APPENDIX E: Don't Mount Up Your Horse (Lyrics) 109

Nothing Can Compare to Eternity (Lyrics) 110

APPENDIX F: Miracles 113

The Greatest Gift (Poem) 114

All by the Power of Jesus (Poem) 115

Introduction

Miracles happen to us every day, yet sometimes we need to open our hearts and minds to see them. There is no secret formula for miracles, because the Bible tells us how to have our prayers answered. I never kept a prayer diary but I wish I did because I might have included a few more memories.

This book is about the miracles in my life I remember the most. I hope and pray that those who read or listen to my stories will have many more miracles than I have had. When we put Jesus first in our lives, there's no telling what or how many miracles God will bring us.

Romans 11:33, "Oh the depth of the riches both of the wisdom and knowledge of God! How unsearchable are his judgments, and his ways past finding out!" (KJV)

My Beginnings

M y name is Terry Price. I'm directly related to "John Price the Immigrant," who came to the Jamestown Colony in 1611 on the ship called "Starr." Records show that he survived the Jamestown Massacre of 1622. It is believed that his house was burned down by the Indians. His wife, Mary, may have died three years before that time but no Prices appear in the list of those who died in the massacre. I found that I am the 13th generation in my family line to live in America through him.

I was born on October 30, 1954, to Carroll and Barbara Price on a snowy Saturday morning in Jefferson City, Missouri at St. Mary's Hospital. I was born with flat feet and I inherited this defect from Mom's father, Clella Smith. (He received his name from General McClellan, who fought against General Lee in the Civil War.)

As soon as I could walk, I had to wear correction shoes. They were white high-top shoes with arch supports. They built my arches a little and helped me so that I could have better blood circulation in my feet.

We moved to Columbia, Missouri when I was about one year old. We lived right on the University of Columbia campus on Lowry Street across from the library. It was a two-story white house next to the campus bookstore. Today, there's a McDonald's Restaurant where our house stood.

When I was three, my family and I moved to Buena Park, California. A year after that, I was playing baseball with my twin friends, Keith and Dale Dennemeyer, that lived next door. One of them hit the ball and it hit me in my right eye. Mom sent me to the doctor and I ended up having to wear an eye patch. I had to wear it for several days and stay indoors before I went back to our doctor.

He removed it and said to Mom, "He should be all right, now!"

I was really glad to have it removed so I could go out and play again. I didn't care what the twins did to me. I thought that they were the best boys in the neighborhood. I noticed that they didn't want to play with me much anymore but I still wanted to play with them. After all, it was just an accident.

My brother, Tony, who was four years older than me, always seemed to have a lot of friends. There were a few boys in the neighborhood he played with, including the twins older brother. He was a good-looking boy, so some of the girls liked him, too.

When I was in Kindergarten, I was in Mrs. Hunter's class. The twins were in my class, so it felt good that they were there, too. I didn't get into too much trouble that year and only got spanked once by the teacher. She disciplined me for hiding behind the piano where she couldn't see me when we were singing.

After I finished that year of school, Mom got me some "Dick and Jane" books to help me to do better in the first grade. She did this because she felt my grades in kindergarten were low. These books also taught me about friendship, which I really needed. They kept me inside a lot and this also helped to prevent me from getting into more trouble the rest of the summer.

When I entered my first grade class, I didn't recognize anyone except Sheri Dailey, who lived in my neighborhood.

I thought *This is really strange that things happened this way. There are several kids my age that live in my neighborhood and she was the only one in my class.* Sheri wasn't a good friend of mine, but we did talk a little. My grades were pretty good and I got along with the teacher, at least.

When summer came, I was playing with a couple boys, in my garage, who lived on the opposite side of the twins. I was happy to have gained two more friends who lived close to me.

The boys were about ages eight and ten, when we each took turns getting into my family's deep freezer which was no longer in use. Once you got into it, the only way you could get out was by someone on the outside opening the door.

When it was my turn, the boys closed the door and I could hear, "I hear Mom calling, we gotta go home."

I realized that I was alone and the freezer was locked. Mom was in the kitchen at the time with a door that separated the kitchen from the garage.

I banged on the inside several times yelling, "Get me out of here!"

Mom heard me and knew we were playing in the garage. It sounded to her like my screams were coming from the freezer.

She came quickly, opened the door and asked, "How did you get in here?"

I told her, "I was playing with the boys next door, and we were taking turns getting into it. I heard one of them yelling and then they left."

I believe the Lord was looking out for me because if my mother wasn't in the kitchen, she never would have heard me. I would have suffocated and died after several more minutes. They didn't come over to play with me after that. (I didn't know it at the time, but this incident caused me to be claustrophobic.)

A few days later I decided to go over to their house to see if they could play. As far as I was concerned, I had two new friends. I didn't care about what they did to me.

When I knocked on their door, their mother answered.

I asked her if her sons could come out to play and she replied, "They're not home."

After she said that, she closed the door and I never saw those boys again. I had forgiven them and didn't hold a grudge against them, since I believed that they didn't do it on purpose.

Since we lived in a cul-de-sac, I played in the street a lot. One day, I got a large cardboard box, pulled it into the street and got inside it. A man was driving his car, saw the box and almost ran over me.

He yelled from his car, "Where do you live?"

I pointed and replied, "In that house over there."

He pulled over, got out of his car, went to my house and told Mom that he almost hit me.

After the man left, Mom yelled, "Terry, get out of the street and put that box up!"

So, I did. I don't remember playing with that box again after that happened. For me, it was as if I was in my own little world escaping from the present world's problems when I was in that box.

I realize, today, that I need to escape from this world, not by using drugs and alcohol but by spending time with God. Today, I can escape into God's world by going into a closet or in my car to talk to God in prayer.

I wanted to be friends with Keith and Dale, but they still seemed unfriendly for some reason. They did enjoy playing by themselves, so I let that be the reason why they acted as they did.

One day, a boy who lived a few houses away from us, on a street corner, started bullying my friends.

I went to his house and he sternly said to me, "Keep off my property, or I'll beat you up!"

I thought *Maybe Keith and Dale will like me more if I beat up this bully*, so I beat him up! He wasn't much of a fighter because all he did was block my punches with his hands.

After a few punches, he said, "Stop it! Stop it! Will you be my friend?"

As much as I wanted friends, I didn't want him to be one. I didn't want to associate with bullies. This didn't seem to help bring more friendship with the twins, but the boy did quit being a bully around us. He tried to hang around with me, so I paid him little attention.

Another time, I played a little rough with a younger boy in my neighborhood, swinging him around. This made him mad and he went home crying to his father (even though I didn't hurt him.) I was afraid his father would come out looking for me, so I ran home. I had found I was home alone, so I hid under Tony's, bed. I was so scared that I peed in my pants.

One of the neighbor girls saw me running home. The father asked her where I lived and she took him into my house. (I didn't think to lock the door.) He found me, pulled me out from under the bed and spanked me.

No miracles happened with this incident, but, to me, it was a miracle that l he didn't harm me more than what he did. However, I learned that if I do something wrong, I need to repent and ask God to "lock the door" (protect me) to prevent Satan from entering and bring harm to me.

I again got into trouble by getting into my dad's jeep. I climbed into it, accidentally hit the gear shift, and went down the inclined driveway out onto the street. Keith and Dale's mother was the first to find out when she went outside. As soon as she saw it, she went to my house, got the keys, and drove it back up the driveway.

I did a lot of things that I shouldn't have been doing that kept Mom "on her toes" all the time. Mom started calling me "Ter-Ter the Terrible." After she told me that, I tried to not be so "terrible" anymore.

Going into the second grade, I noticed that Sheri was again the only one in my classroom that lived near me. I was upset because I wanted others from my neighborhood there, so I could impress them by studying hard and doing well on the class work and tests.

I didn't ask anyone why things turned out the way they did. I just thought that it was done on purpose by Mom. I was too mad to ask her about it. In fact, for a few months, it affected my behavior in school. I can't remember what I did, but my grades were not as good as they should have been. Therefore, I didn't like my teacher, Mrs. Cherry, even though it really *wasn't* Mom's decision to put me in her class.

Sheri Daily was assigned to sit next to me the first day of school. She was a pretty girl and was always polite with the teacher. She wore nice clothes and her hair was always nicely done. To me, she was a model student and I wanted to act as good as she did.

A few days later, she was moved to another class, (probably to balance the number of kids in each classroom.) This made me mad that now I had no friends in my class and I felt lonely. I thought *Why should I try so hard to do good in this class? I don't have any friends to show that I can do good.*

I couldn't run more than a block without feeling really tired. When I came home from school, I had to lie on my back and lift my legs up in the air in order to get the circulation back in my legs. I found that I could get around on my tricycle without getting tired so quickly. I made it my main transportation to go all over the neighborhood.

One school day, Tony showed me a shortcut to get to school by a dairy farm. Sometimes I walked to school by myself and took the shortcut. Since I didn't like school, I didn't care about arriving on time. I would stop and call the cows to me by saying "sue cow, sue cow" until they came close and this would have made me late for school if I didn't run. Since running was difficult for me, I had to do it in spurts.

How God Taught Me Humility

D uring the summer, we went to Huntington Beach, which was a short drive. When I was playing in the waves I noticed a sign floating in the water. I reached over and picked it up. It was a small wooden sign with the words "Port Said" on it. It had floated all the way from Egypt.

As we loaded up our F85 Oldsmobile, I thought of all of the fame I could have. I thought *Maybe I could get in the newspaper and have my picture taken or be on TV.*

I put the sign in our back yard where I kept an eye on it while I played there.

When it was getting late, Mom called me inside, "Terry, it's time to come inside and get ready for bed!"

I thought she said, "Terry, leave the sign outside and get ready for bed."

So, I left it outside trying to be obedient to her.

When I went to bed, I had a dream. In it, I was in a parade riding in a convertible, waving my hand at the crowds. The Salvation Army Band was in front of me playing two songs, "When the Saints Go Marching In" and "76 Trombones." I really started to get a lot of pride in my heart.

The next day, I went outside to see the sign and it was gone. I never believed that Tony could have taken it somewhere because I really

7

trusted him. After all, he is my brother. I do remember, though, that Tony was gone the whole day with his friends.

This reminded me, later in life, of Job 1:21 "The Lord gave, and the Lord has taken away." (NKJV)

I believe that the Lord took it away from me to help keep me from being puffed up with pride. My little boy dreams were stolen away!

Proverbs 16:18 says, "Pride goes before destruction, and a haughty spirit before a fall." (NKJV)

For the next few days, I checked the newspaper to see if someone else claimed to have found it. I found nothing. I thought about the person who might have stolen it and realized he wouldn't want it to be publicized because he would be found out. I learned that the thief has less value for what he steals than the one who originally owned it. I didn't *want* to know if Tony might have taken it because I didn't want to have any reason to be mad at him. I loved and trusted him since he *is* my brother.

I was only in second grade for a few months before we moved to Long Beach, California. I was glad about moving because I didn't like my teacher. Tony came to pick me up from my class the day that we left. I was happy to see him, but as I left the room, I saw Mrs. Cherry and stuck my tongue out at her.

She put her hands on her hips and had a mean look on her face. All the students turned and looked at me in silence. I didn't care what they thought at that moment because I knew that I was never coming back!

Tony saw this and yanked me away from the door. He asked, "Did you get everything you needed out of the classroom?"

I replied, "Yes!"

He chuckled, "Good because I'm not going back <u>there</u> again!"

Maybe I'll make a new friend in the new school and have a better teacher, too!

Before we moved, my report card that I got in second grade, showed a "D" in conduct and a "C" for everything else.

Mrs. Cherry wrote these words on my report card: "Terry wastes a good deal of time when he is given time to work. He is capable of doing much more. He must learn to be more responsible."

I got off to a bad start with my new second grade teacher, Ms. Coy. I was really tired one day from staying up late from all of the moving we did. I yawned in her class and said, "Ho-Hum."

When I did this, the teacher put her hands on her hips and said, "OK, who yawned?"

I didn't answer because I didn't know what the word meant, but many of the students in the class pointed at <u>me</u>. It was at that moment I learned a new word.

She said with a stern voice, "OK, Terry, go stand out in the hallway, I'll come out and talk to you in a few minutes."

I had no idea how much trouble I was in, and all I knew was that I said "Ho-Hum" from being so tired.

She came out and scolded me, "I will not have you yawning in my class, so you will stay out here until I say you can come back in the classroom!"

After I cried for about fifteen minutes, I became angry and quit crying. With my back against the wall, I put my right foot on it and just stood in the hallway with my arms folded. For another fifteen minutes, I stuck out my lower lip, wondering what I had done that was so wrong. I watched the clock on the wall across from me, and it seemed like a very long time.

I even thought *There is probably no one in the class who likes me now. Maybe I should see Principal Rolo and talk to him about what happened,* but then I thought *I might get into trouble with Ms. Coy if I leave.*

I couldn't defend myself because I didn't understand what was going on.

While I was out in the hallway, the school called my mother and told her about it. She told them I probably yawned because I had to stay up late the night before since I helped move and waited for my family to set up my bed.

Finally, she came out and told me, "OK, you can come back in my class now!"

A couple weeks later, I did another thing to make things worse, which caused even more regret. The teacher announced that we were going to play charades.

This might be my chance to impress the kids in my class.

She asked if anyone would volunteer to start the game and show us how to do it. I raised my hand and so did a few others. (I really didn't want to be picked, I just wanted my class to think that I knew how to play the game.)

Mrs. Coy said, "OK, Terry why don't you be first and show us how to play the game."

I reluctantly went to the front of the class and pulled a slip of paper out of a small box. The paper read, "Salute the flag."

Since I had no idea what I was doing, I read it out loud, "Salute the flag."

Some of the children said, "That's not how you play the game."

I got embarrassed and the teacher said, "Would someone else like to do it?"

I quietly sat down and another student was picked to take my place. The others got up and played the game right while I quietly sat back, too ashamed of myself to participate.

A few weeks later, Mrs. Coy taught us how to square dance and she asked us to pair up, one boy with one girl.

I saw two girls fight over who had to pair with me.

The first girl said to the other, "I don't want to dance with him, you dance with him!"

The other girl replied, "No, I don't want to, you dance with him!"
One of the boys in my class told the first girl, "I'll dance with you!"
The first girl said, "See, I already have a dance partner!"
The other girl said reluctantly, "OK, I'll dance with Terry."

I was glad that I got a partner and she was a girl, too. I did my best to try to impress her. She seemed to be a good dancer and she was good looking. She never looked at me but at everyone else. This made me realize I didn't have any real friends in my class, so I got even more upset about being there and even in the whole school. I developed stage fright after this, because of the way I embarrassed myself in front of the class.

In third grade, there were all new students in my class, so it gave me a fresh start and I knew I had to, because I had to make new friends, if I wanted any. I made friends with a classmate named Chris Hetlinger and sometimes I went to his house on my way home and played in his back yard in a big tree that had a rope swing. He was one of the best friends I ever had. Thanks to our friendship, adjusting to life was a lot easier for me!

Chris and I were in Cub Scouts together so we had even more time to hang around with each other. Mom was our Den Mother and Tony was our Den Chief because he was in Boy Scouts. When it came to earning achievements, Chris was ahead of all of us. I thought of him as an over-achiever and I wanted to be like that, too.

One of the worst things happened to me when I was in the 4th grade. One boy told me, "You're the ugliest person in this school."

I told him in anger, "You have an ugly mouth!"

At the age of 9, I was gullible and believed what he said. I told my teacher, Mrs. Cox, about it and all she said to him was, "Don't do that again!"

I was surprised that it was all she said to him, but it was better than nothing. This made me realize how easy it was to hurt people with words. I understood better why we should say nice things to others. You never know when someone might need a kind word. I made it a point, from then on, to try to always be nice to other people.

It was several problems like this that seemed to add to my stage fright I developed over the years. I started having bad thoughts about myself. I thought I was ugly because I had a lot of freckles. I also thought I was a bad kid no one wanted to play with, except for Chris.

I Samuel 16:7 says, "...for man looks on the outward appearance, but the LORD looks at the heart." (NKJV) I learned God doesn't care what I look like and one day when I go to heaven I would have a perfect body.

On August 7, 1963, T.J., my brother, was born. I was glad to have a brother and I determined to spend time to play with him when I got home from school. I wanted him to become my best friend and someone fun to hang around with.

It was in 5th grade when I went to our family doctor, Dr. Ogata, who worked on getting my arches built up. The doctor wrapped my feet in plaster to get a mold of my arch, and on my next visit he gave me specially designed plastic arch supports. He also had me do exercises to help strengthen my arches.

All of these experiences helped me to learn humility, and by them, I learned the first step to having answers to prayer. I began to learn to esteem others more than myself.

One good experience I had was with my Dad. He had served in the Army National Guard, and as a Military Police Captain, he was chosen to be one of the first Polygraph Examiners. When he began teaching Police Science at Long Beach State College, he taught how to use the lie detector. (He even used the lie detector on me.) Dad and his lie detector taught me the value of telling the truth.

Most of all, I knew that the Bible taught me not to lie. My Sunday school teachers taught me that Exodus 20:16 tells us, "You shall not bear false witness against your neighbor." (KJV)

A New Beginning and a Changed Life

W e moved to Upland, California, and my doctor appointments were discontinued. However, upon entering sixth grade, I was able to do activities with my classmates without any foot problems. For the first time, I was able to do the 600 yard run.

I was proud I was able to go that distance without any real pain in my feet, and my legs didn't feel heavy after running. However, I had to walk a portion of it, since I had never run that far before.

My classmates saw I was a slow runner, so when we did a relay race between the boys and girls, I was chosen as the anchor man. Since I was the last one to carry the baton, I felt I had to prove the boys could beat the girls.

When the girls found out I was the anchor, the two tallest ones fought over who would run against me. Fortunately, I was a little faster than the fastest girl, and we won the relay race. (I probably wouldn't have lived it down if I lost the race for our team.)

While in sixth grade, I got into fights with a couple boys who were in my class. They were two bullies who fought with me on my way home. I didn't want to report them, because I was afraid that the principal would expel all of us. (This was usually the way schools handled things in those days.)

After sixth grade, we moved to a different house in town. I went to

Pioneer Junior High and attended Ontario First Baptist Church. At the church, Pastor Authelet gave an invitation for people who wanted to be saved so I went forward.

Doing this became a real turning point in my life. I started loving others more and gave more devotion to God. This was the first and most important event in my life. I applied John 15:12 which says, "This is my commandment, that you love one another, as I have loved you." (NKJV)

A pamphlet the church gave me, said I should start praying for my future wife. I believed God knows everything even about our future. Therefore, I knew God knows who I was to marry and everything about her. I found out, later after we married, she really did need my prayers in that time of her life.

Junior High was a time I was able to strengthen my legs and feet because I was involved in several sports in the physical education classes. I found out I could wrestle pretty well because it didn't require a lot of standing or running. I wasn't too interested in this sport, so I chose not to do it when I got out of junior high.

In my physical education class, our coach asked, "Is there anyone who hasn't had a chance to be a team leader in baseball, yet?"

I, with about three others, raised our hands. The coach told us to pick our teams.

I'm going to use my faith in God to pick a winning team.

Then I chose the batting order, and I put who I thought were the best players first with myself last. I also put my best friend, Steve, as the fourth batter, (known as the clean-up man,) because he was a good hitter and his uncle just happened to be a professional baseball player.

Half of the way through the game, our team managed to load the bases and it was Steve's turn at bat. He was a little on the heavy side, so we yelled, "Put your weight into it."

To my delight, he hit a grand-slam home run and we ended up

winning the game. I considered this to be an answer to prayer, and it helped increase my faith in God. To me, it was a miracle.

My life began to really change. I had received Jesus, who is the best Friend a person could have. I became a friendlier person and gained a few friends.

I learned this lesson: If you want to gain friends, get them to laugh *with* you. If you want to lose friends, get them to laugh *at* you.

Proverbs 18:24 says, "A man who has friends must himself be friendly, but there is a friend who sticks closer than a brother." (NKJV)

My Miracle Cure

I'm one of those people who get the hick-ups easily. One morning, after eating too fast, I got the hick-ups and they wouldn't stop. I tried a lot of things to get rid of them. I held my breath as long as I could, drank water, put a bag over my head, and tried to scare them away. Nothing worked! I went to bed still having the hick-ups.

The next morning, I woke up with the same problem for another six hours. I finally decided to pray them away. The moment after I asked the Lord to take them away, my hick-ups were completely gone!

Matthew 8:13 says, "And Jesus said to the centurion, Go your way; and as you have believed, so be it done to you. And his servant was healed the selfsame hour."

Running Cross Country and Track

When I entered Upland High School, I noticed they had a cross country team that ran a two mile run. I decided to try out for it because I thought it would be a really good way to strengthen my arches. I also thought I could also outrun any bullies like I had in the sixth grade.

The first day that the cross country team met, Coach Robert Loney talked to us about the coming season and the courses we had to run. He also told us that we would have to run the whole distance without walking in the time trial we had to do the next day, in order to be on the team.

He said, "If you've never run the course before, I would advise you to run it today, so that you will know the route to take in the time trial."

I decided to run the course and as I did, I found that I had to walk some of it. I determined to do my best because I didn't want to lose sight of the runners in front of me. Towards the end, I did lose sight of them, but I knew enough about the school that I found my way to the finish line that was at the football field where we started.

The next day, I prayed and asked the Lord to help me to run the whole two miles, and to my surprise, I was able to run the whole distance with a time of 15 minutes and 55 seconds in the time trial. Out of 55 runners, I was in last place, but I made the team and God answered my prayer.

The first day of practice, we were to run seven miles. We had to run down a semi-deserted street to the Cucamonga Wash and back. I already knew that I couldn't run the whole distance but I would give it a good try. One thing Coach told us that helped was to shorten our stride on the up-hills and to lengthen our stride on the down-hills.

As I was running I thought to myself *Why do they call this practice? After all, I am running now. Well, maybe more like jogging and walking, but I doubt that I will be running much faster than this in our first meet!*

As I was about a mile away from the wash, I noticed a couple of runners who had already turned around and were heading back. I turned around and went with them; because I was sure I couldn't go the whole distance and be back before they closed the locker room (or so I thought.) I prayed to the Lord that He would help me do my best.

One of the runners said, "You need to run the whole way. You're just cheating yourself if you don't!"

"I'm too worn out to make it, I'm just glad I could make it this far."

So, I ran back with them part of the way and they ended up leaving me behind. I was glad that I was able to go as far as I did and thanked the Lord for it.

As the days progressed, I was able to run farther and without walking any of the distance. Sometimes, I would run to an elementary school which was eight miles round trip or to the dam and back which was ten. The school had drinking fountains that I drank from so it encouraged me to run there to quench my thirst.

The Lord impressed upon my heart to run the first part (about a mile) a little faster than my average pace. When I got too tired to keep up the pace, I slowed down to a slow jog. As I got my strength back, I increased my pace back to what it was. I would keep running this way until I was about a mile from the school and then I would run as fast as I was able.

I always ran by myself because of the way I was running. I felt that if I ran with someone then one of us would not be training as hard as the other. It was lonely to run that way but I was able to have time with the Lord, singing songs in my heart and thinking of Bible verses. A couple of those songs were "Footsteps of Jesus" and "Trust and Obey."

One of the verses I thought about was Hebrews 12:1, "Wherefore, seeing we also are compassed about with so great a cloud of witnesses, let us lay aside every weight, and the sin which does so easily beset us, and let us run with patience the race that is set before us." I mainly repeated to myself the last few words of the verse.

The day before the meet, we would jog a mile (warm-up), do ten wind-sprints and end with a mile jog (warm-down.) We did these sprints from one goal post to the other on the football field. We would sprint one way and jog back without stopping.

I followed these two rules:

(1) Change your pace when training

(2) Run an even pace when you're racing

The first race we did was against Eisenhower High School and my time improved by close to a minute and a half. It felt good that I did so well and I wasn't in last place this time.

My second race was a course in the foothills of a mountain at Webb High School, which I ran with a time of 16:05. I was last again, but this was a course Coach told us about that our times would be slower. This was a very hilly race, so I wasn't bothered by the slower time. I was glad I was able to run up and down those hills without walking any of it.

I improved on my time as the season progressed and at the end, I ran with a time of 11:33, which is an improvement of 4 minutes and 22 seconds. Now I was running in the middle of the pack!

During the cross country season, I decided to run up to a mountain village which was 12 miles from my house. I had a friend who lived there named Brian. I ran all the way up to his house in Baldy Village. Being thirsty, I knocked on his door, and when he opened it, he looked surprised to see me.

Then I said to him, "Hi, Brian, I ran up here for about 13 miles. Could you give me some water, please?"

"How about I give you some Kool Aid?" he said with a smile, "I can't let you come inside, because I'm the only one home right now."

I told him, "That's OK, Brian, I can't stay long anyways."

He went inside and returned with a pitcher full of the drink and a cup for me to use. When he gave them to me, I drank it down fast, and he filled up my cup again.

After I finished the whole pitcher, I told him, "I'm still thirsty."

Brian said, "Wow!" and went to get another pitcher full.

When he brought that pitcher to me, I drank it down, too.

I then realized that I had to run back home, so I asked him, "Do you know of anyone who is going back down to Upland?"

He replied, "No."

"Well, it looks like I'll be running back home, since I have no one to take me

there!"

"Good luck!" he said.

"Thanks for the drink, I feel better now! See you later!"

I ran back to the high school, which was another 13 miles, but, downhill. I forced myself to slow down, because my feet were going so fast that I could barely keep my balance on the steep road.

When I got to the high school, my legs felt like rubber and my arches hurt. What made things more difficult was that I had to walk a mile back to my house and it was painful to walk.

For about three days after, I could barely run because of the pain in my feet and the soreness in my legs. Fortunately, I ran on a Friday, so

I had time to recover before the following Monday when I had to run again. I did the foot exercises I had learned in the past and it ended up being about three weeks before I completely recovered.

The officials took the top five players of our team and our best running times in the state meet to determine how we ranked in the nation. Our cross country team took first place in Southern California and fifth in the nation. The varsity team competed at the same college where Dad used to teach in Long Beach for the C.I.F. championship.

My freshman-sophomore team, took third in the nation that year. I may have been the seventh fastest runner on the team, but at least I can say that I was on a winning team. (I managed to get a trophy, too!) That year, I also ran the two mile run and the 1320 yard run in track. I was the slowest runner in the 1320, however, my time did improve in the two mile event. My best two mile time was 11:19 by the end of the season.

The following summer, I got to run a half-marathon race at the Fontana Days Marathon in Fontana, California. Since it's a 13.1 mile downhill race, it's called the fastest course in the world. Our high school cross country coach was with the few of us who came from our team and he believed that we could run this race, so that's good enough for me! I figured that I could run it without too much trouble, because they had water stations along the way and free food at the finish line.

This race had a winding road at the beginning and was filled with many other runners from ages 10 to 87. I ran next to an 87-year-old man and talked to him for about the first mile of the race.

I was impressed that he was running this race and I thought, *I hope that I can run this race when I get to be his age!*

Then I realized my pace felt a little slow so I began to run a little faster. I decided, instead of making this a run for fun, I should run my best. I was able to finish the race with a time of 81 minutes and 55 second.

I was so tired afterward, that I laid on my back for several minutes until I got some of my strength back. It felt like my arches may have fallen during the race and cut off some of the circulation, so it ended up being another three days before I could run again.

After summer, I went to Center High School in Kansas City, Missouri. I joined their cross country team and my time continued to improve.

By my junior year, I was the fastest runner on the team. Then, I became a cross country co-captain in my senior year, and took first place in a few cross country meets, with my best time being 10:35.

I also did the two mile run with the track team as I had done in Upland and my running time was even faster in track, since I ran on a flat surface. In my junior year, I broke the Junior Varsity record in the District Meet, and a year later, my best two mile time was 10:12.8. In my senior year, I was able to take first place in several meets in track.

I Corinthians 9:24 says, "Do you not know that they which run in a race run all, but one receives the prize? So run, that ye may obtain." (KJV)

I Corinthians 10:31 says, "Whether therefore you eat, or drink, or whatsoever you do, do all to the glory of God." (KJV) I believed I did it for God's glory and not my own.

Praying I Could Do My Best

As I always did, I prayed I would do my best when I ran, instead of trying to beat a certain time. As the season went on, in my Senior year, I believed, by doing my best I would run much faster. I was better at running two miles instead of running one. (During the indoor season, the longest running event was the one mile run.)

In a race near the end of the season, I thought of running the first half of the mile faster, hoping the last half would be fast, also. As I was running, I was just a few yards behind my friend Mike Bickle.

I spoke loudly while trying to catch my breath, "Come on, Mike, pick up your pace, I'm right behind you."

I found myself slowly falling behind, because I couldn't keep up the pace to encourage him on. I did run one of my better races, but I found myself bombarded by comments for doing it.

Coach Forrest Arnall, who was also my cross country coach, said, "You're just trying to beat Mike!"

I replied with what breath I could, "No I wasn't, Coach!"

I heard the same thing from the other runners, "You're just trying to beat Mike!"

I told them, as I was still trying to catch my breath, "No, I wasn't!"

They were convinced I was, but I knew I wasn't and that was all that mattered to me. I knew that God was only interested in me doing my best and that's what I did.

A few days later, I suffered from a knee injury running in the hallways at school during indoor track practice, so it ruined any chance of being able to get a scholarship to go to college. I had to run two miles in under ten minutes during regular track season to qualify. I was finding it more difficult to improve my running to make that goal.

I learned from my running experiences about having limits and I was not invincible. I had pushed myself beyond my limits a few times and suffered for it. I also learned I could get badly injured going beyond those limits.

During my senior year, I found that I had many friends. I guess it was because of my accomplishments. I had several students say, "Hi, Terry" to me in the hallways in school that I didn't even know. This was a real change from my younger years when I had only a few friends. I also applied the Bible verse to my life that says in John 15:12, "This is my commandment, That you love one another as I have loved you." (KJV)

Even though Mike Bickle went to a different church than me, I hung around with him because I believed he would be a good influence on me. He said that he was going to be a preacher someday. He was one year behind me in school and played football on the varsity team.

One day he came up to me with a few of his other friends and said, "I'm getting ready to be a preacher, so I can't date girls right now so I can only hang around with you guys, because you're Christians."

I said to him, "That's alright, as long as we go ice skating, because we all could use the exercise to help us to run better in track."

One of the others said, "Are you sure we can't bring a girlfriend with us?"

Mike replied, "They won't allow me to do that. Come on you guys, will you help me out?"

I said to Mike, "We're only going ice skating, right?"

"If that's what you guys want to do!"

We all reluctantly agreed and said, "OK," since we knew we needed the exercise.

After all, it was only for a few hours, so we did have the opportunity to date girls at other times. (I never saw Mike again after my senior year, but I heard that he went on to preach at the International House of Prayer in the south part of Kansas City, Missouri.)

In my senior year, the boys had track practice with the girls, too! I wasn't good at sprinting, in fact, I was probably the slowest runner in any of the short distances. This was because I didn't want to hurt my arches and end up having difficulty running, again. (I had learned this in my freshman year.)

When we were running the 220 yard dash in practice, I noticed two girls were fighting over who would run against me. I guess, by now, I was used to girls fighting over me but I knew I could still beat them.

When one girl was ready to run against me, the other girl said, "Let me run against him!"

The other replied, "No, I want to!"

I'm a faster runner than you!"

"Oh, all right!"

I ran against the faster one and she was right behind me for the first 110 yards. On the last stretch, I beat her by about 2 or 3 seconds. The girls didn't try running against me after that, and I was glad because I couldn't risk being teased by the other runners. I never was good in the sprinting events, but I ended up being the third fastest runner Center High ever had in the two mile run.

When it came time to graduate from high school, I had one class I was doing poorly in, but it was required for graduation. I was making a "F" in English Literature. I didn't care for that class, because I didn't think it was necessary for anything in the future.

The teacher told us, in order for a few of us to pass in her class we had to make an "E" on our final. (An "E" was the highest grade.) I studied real hard for that test and had more time since track season was over. I also did a lot of praying.

I made an E minus on the test, which had me worried, since it wasn't an "E." I found out the day before graduation that I had passed the class. What a relief that was! I wasn't about to go to summer school just to repeat a class that I didn't like. I took to heart the verse in Psalms 55:17 that says, "Evening, and morning and at noon will I pray, and cry aloud: and he shall hear my voice." (KJV)

Longview Community College

After high school, I attended Longview Community College in Lee's Summit, Missouri and majored in Architecture. My Dad was the Dean of the Metropolitan Junior College District in the Kansas City area, so I was able to get a discount on my tuition.

I found I didn't do well with artistic drawings. I needed this ability to help me to do well as an architect. I decided to go ahead and finish the classes, even if it meant getting lower grades, to get some college credits. I also decided to pay more attention in my Math and English classes.

While I was there, I met a friend named David Jaeger, who went to another Baptist Church. I learned my family was moving to a place that was closer to his church.

The Lord was convicting my heart to serve Him. The church that I was presently attending didn't have any ministry that I was interested in at the time. I thought about having a puppet ministry, but I didn't have the money to buy any puppets. I also thought about being involved in a bus ministry.

Wanting to serve the Lord was the second most important event in my life. The Lord was convicting me about going to another church that had these kind of outreach ministries I could do.

I started going to TriCity Baptist Church, where David attended.

I told Mom about the church and she started going there, too. She also brought T.J. with her and got involved in working in the church's day care center. It felt good that I wasn't going to church by myself as I had done for a few years.

It was now nice to go to church. I took to heart Psalms 133:1, "Behold, how good and how pleasant it is for brethren to dwell together in unity." (KJV)

It was around this time that Mom and Dad divorced, so Mom began to read her Bible and making friends in church which helped her through her problems.

We were living in Raytown, Missouri, when Dad left Mom. It wasn't devastating to me as much as it was for my brother T.J., who was eleven years old.

After the divorce, he kept asking Mom, "Do you love me?"

Mom always replied, "Yes, I love you."

The divorce made T.J. feel insecure and I felt sorry for him. I was busy with college, so it was difficult for me to spend time with him. Tony was on his own, married to a pretty lady named Nancy, and living in California working with the Los Angeles Police Department.

T.J.'s response reminded me of the fact that sometimes we act like God is miles away looking in on us occasionally. But, I believe He is always there standing right beside us with unconditional love, watching and hearing everything we say and do.

Proverbs 15:3 says, "The eyes of the Lord are in every place, keeping watch on the good and the evil." (NKJV)

Twin Miracles

T riCity had a good visitation program and they even had one for the teens. I went out on church visitation several times and I always enjoyed having my friend Charley, as my partner. He was a devout Christian teenager, from a Bible Church, who said he would become a youth director someday. Every time we went on visitation, we always managed to lead someone to the Lord.

One day when we were together, I told him that I felt led by the Lord to go visit an old high school friend of mine named Steve. I knew that he had Christian values, but I wasn't sure he was saved.

When we got to his house, he answered the door. I asked if we could come in and he said we could, but he had a couple of his twin cousins from Springfield visiting him.

I asked Steve if he was a born again Christian and he said he was. Then I asked him about his cousins if we could talk to them. He said we could, so he let us in and Charley talked to one of them and I talked to the other. They both got saved!

Charley and I both agreed that this was of the Lord when we went to see Steve. We were only expecting to see him. Both of us got to see two miracle rebirths that night!

Luke 15:7 says, "I say to you, that likewise joy shall be in heaven over one sinner that repents, more than over ninety and nine just persons, which need no repentance." (KJV) I know the angels were rejoicing twice as much and so were we! I believe our highest calling is to point people to Jesus.

In church, the teens were given points for each time they did a ministry during the summer. If we reached a certain number of points by the end of summer, we could go to Six Flags Over St. Louis for free. I saw that I was the only one who had accumulated enough points. I got prideful about it and ended up with the flu the day before we left.

As the day progressed, I was getting over the flu and just feeling weak. I decided to go anyway and hoped that by lying down in the aisle of the bus, I would feel better by the time we got there.

It didn't make me any feel better and I had to go on the rides by myself, since no one wanted to take a chance on catching my flu. I felt really lightheaded on the rides, but it made it a new experience for me. I was still weak on the way home, so I still had to lie on the floor of the bus. I had to learn again that pride goes before a fall (or my case, a "lying down.")

Miracles at Tennessee Temple College

I decided that it would be best for me to go to a four-year college, where I could earn a Bachelor's Degree in Secondary Education. I prayed about which college I should go to and the Lord impressed upon my heart to go to Tennessee Temple College in Chattanooga, Tennessee.

I was planning on going to Temple in the fall. I didn't know for sure if I could go until a week before I left. I tried to save up as much money as I could and went on faith that the Lord would supply the rest. I prayed that I would have enough money to enroll and quickly get a job. At least, I didn't have enough time to get a lot of pride about going off to college.

I traveled by a Greyhound Bus and it took several hours before I got there. This would be the first time that I would leave home and be by myself. I felt all alone and concerned that all would go well for me. I prayed about it and it seemed to help, because I realized that wherever I am, God is always with me. I had to rely more on God and less on people.

Hebrews 13:5 says, "Let your conversation be without covetousness; and be content with such things as you have: for he has said, I will never leave you, nor forsake you." (KJV)

When I arrived at the bus depot, there was a man who came with a college van and said, "If anyone is going to Tennessee Temple College, I have a van waiting outside."

When we got in the van, we started getting acquainted with one another and asking where each of us were from and a little about ourselves. Since everyone seemed so friendly, I felt it wouldn't be hard for me to make friends. Going by van was more fun and I didn't have to pay for a taxi. It was important to me to have as much of my money as possible to go towards tuition and books.

I discovered I had more than enough money to get registered and I went to my new dorm which was called Phillips Hall. I found my dorm room and saw two clothes closets that were empty. I noticed that two other people had been in the room earlier and claimed their beds and closets. Of the two closets left and I saw one that was wider than the other, so I took the widest one.

The last roommate came in and told me his name and asked for mine.

I told him, "My name is Terry Price."

"You'll have to take all of your things out of that closet and put it in the other one, because I have been here longer than you. I was in this room last year, so I have seniority."

I, then, put my clothes into the smaller one and I noticed that they barely fit with about four inches of space left. When he put his clothes into the wider closet, I noticed that his clothes only fit into about half of its space.

When he left to visit with friends, I put my left hand on the left side of the closet and my right hand on my suit coats, and I prayed over my clothes that I might have more of them. About an hour after I prayed, He came back with another student who had brought in four of his suit jackets with him.

The student looked at me and with an Australian accent he said, "I have to give my jackets away, because they don't fit me anymore. Would you like to have them?"

I responded, "Yes, I was just praying that I would get some new suits!"

As I put them into my closet, I thought *When I prayed I had put my right hand on my suit coats, so maybe I should have put my hand on my pants and dress shirts! I might have gotten them, instead?*

My closet was now crammed full and I had a hard time accepting the fact that people could be that selfish and attend a Christian college.

I told him, "I really need to use the bigger closet now, since I got more clothes!"

He replied with insistence, pointing to his closet, "No, this one is mine!"

"I am a sophomore, because I transferred from another college."

"That doesn't matter, because I was in this room last year so I have seniority!"

I then thought *There was no chance of changing closets at this point with this guy, so I'll just have to adapt to this dorm life*, and I said submissively, "OK, OK!"

A few days later, I got a job on my first attempt. This was an answer to prayer. I had to take a bus to get to work but I didn't mind traveling that way and there were other Temple students that rode the same bus to their jobs.

After attending Tennessee Temple College a few months, I went to a Bible Conference and the speaker talked about doing God's will. He taught that to do His will, I had to put God first in my life and not to give into temptations. I did my best to control my thoughts, to be careful of what I said and read my Bible daily.

I remember hearing about how God will give you the desires of your heart if you do His will, so I took the Lord up on His offer. When I got back to the dorm room, I told myself *I love coconut, and I haven't had any in a long time. I know the Lord will give me some if I ask for it.* I then prayed saying, "Lord please forgive me of my sins and please give me some coconut. In Jesus' name, amen." As I was praying, one of my roommates, Rodney, heard me when he walked into the room.

Two days later, a student came knocking on our door when my roommates were there and he asked, "Does anyone want some coconut?

I happily replied, "I'd like to have some."

He gave me some of his coconut, just as I asked from the Lord. (He had no idea I had previously prayed for it.) Rodney saw him give me the coconut and was quite surprised about the whole thing.

This reminded me of Matthew 21:22, "And all things whatsoever you shall ask in prayer, believing, you shall receive." (KJV)

I prayed asking the Lord to give me a ministry while I was in college. During the time of registration, I saw people working with puppets. They had an outdoor display where everyone could see them. I went up to them and said that I had an interest in doing puppets, so they signed me on. I ended up working with them for several months.

I believed that this would be good therapy to help overcome my stage fright. I could hide behind a stage while performing with puppets.

A few days after that, God told me these few words, "81st and Park."

The only place that I knew about with that address was in Kansas City, Missouri. A short time later, He also gave me a vision of several children playing on a street corner with a teenage girl, wearing a dress, holding a ball in her hands. All the children looked like they were wearing hand-me-downs. It was as if I were looking at a photograph.

I knew what this would mean! After the school year, I was to go from Chattanooga to Kansas City, Missouri, to my home church and start a bus route there. This would also mean that I would be gone for a summer and a semester.

My only real problem at the time was that I didn't have a car. I prayed for one so that I could visit my bus route. I said to the Lord, "I needed a bronze colored compact car with a manual transmission, stick-shift, bucket seats, white interior and good on gas."

When the school year was coming to an end, my mother told me that Tony was going to give me his car. It surprised Mom that I didn't seem so excited about it. She didn't know I was praying for one, so I could start a bus route when I got home.

Miracles in Kansas City

W hen I got home to Kansas City, my brother gave me his car, an Opel Manta, just as I had prayed for! The only thing was, I forgot to pray for a good running car (as it was in need of repairs.)

The first Sunday I was home, I went to church and told the bus director, that I wanted to start a bus route on the east side of Kansas City. When I told him about the area, he told me that there were a couple families in that part of town that would ride the bus to church if I picked them up.

The Lord spoke to my heart to start visiting the route the following Saturday and to be at the corner of 81st and Park on that day at noon. When I arrived there, I saw 10 children on the very same corner as I saw in my vision with a girl holding a ball. I invited them to come to church, and all of them (from the same family) said that they would come. I also visited the other families that my bus director told me to visit and a few others that I found. They all said that they would come as well. The next day, we had 19 people on the bus.

Within a couple Sundays, five of the children from 81st and Park received Jesus. There were a few others who were saved in the weeks to come that lived on the bus route as well. The route grew over the months as many more children came.

When things like this happen, I believe that someone else is praying for it, too. Perhaps the grandparents of the children in my vision were praying for their salvation.

I had to pray that I could make it to the gas station every week since I didn't make a lot of money working at the Sonic Drive-In Restaurant in Raytown. By the time I got off work on Fridays, I would have less than an eighth of a tank of gas to get me to the bank and then to the closest gas station. It seemed that every time I managed to pull in, I just happened to run out of gas. (One time, I had pulled up too far for the gas pump to reach and the car wouldn't start, so the attendant had to stretch the hose and hold on to it so it would reach my tank.)

There was another time that my car wouldn't start when I was in the church parking lot. Dr. Gary Coleman, a visiting evangelist from Garland, Texas and my pastor Al Cockrell, saw that I was trying to start my car. Dr. Coleman was embarrassed because he couldn't help me since they were on their way to the airport.

Within minutes after they left, my car started right up. I figured that they were praying for me as soon as they got into the car. I was then able to go visit my bus route on that day.

As soon as I had the money, I had the clutch and the clutch plate replaced, costing me about $800. I was a little disappointed because I was in need of that money to help pay towards my tuition. By God's grace, I always managed to get to my bus route. The Lord did supply me with enough money to get my car fixed. I learned to regard the Lord's miracles as that which is given by His merciful kindness. They are all undeserved.

By God's grace, I always managed to get to my bus route. At first, I was discouraged because I needed that money for college. I reminded myself that God gave me that car, so I had no room to complain. Also, a verse came into my mind from Philippians 4:19, "But my God shall supply all your need according to his riches in glory by Christ Jesus." (KJV)

After a few months, the children that came faithfully from 81ˢᵗ and Park, told me their family was going to start attending another Baptist church closer to them, because it was at least a half hour drive to our church. I gave them my blessings and told the children that they needed to do what their parents told them to do. I also explained that it was God's will for them to go to another church with their parents.

I realized the main reason for my being there with the bus route was no longer necessary. Also, there were two other young men who were willing to take over the route.

First Lady Rosalynn Carter

M y dad remarried to a lady named Marge Ford and they lived just north of 50 highway in Kansas City, Missouri. I visited them occasionally while working the bus route. I stayed with Mom and T.J. and we lived two miles from Arrowhead Stadium near Interstate 70, just a few miles from Dad.

One day Dad invited me to go visit First Lady Rosalynn Carter. She was visiting to talk to fellow Democrats about the Equal Rights Amendment. His next-door neighbor, who held a government office, invited all of us to go with them.

We went to the Muelbach Hotel in downtown Kansas City to a meeting room. There was standing room only with no chairs to sit in and a lot of important Democrats in the room. I wondered if I was the only one that wasn't a Democrat.

After Rosalynn gave her speech, everyone applauded. Since I wasn't interested in supporting the Equal Rights Amendment, I only clapped a little and hid behind a man, hoping that no one would see me showing so little interest.

After everyone was finished, I noticed they were starting a line to shake her hand.

Many of them were saying things like, "I will support you on the Equal Rights Amendment."

That made me feel nervous and I slipped to the back of the line. It gave me time to think of what to say, without compromising my beliefs.

I silently prayed to the Lord "Lord help me to say the right thing to her."

The Lord said to me, "Tell her that you will be praying for her."

When it was my turn to shake her hand to offer my support, I said to her with an assuring smile on my face, I'll be praying for you." She looked at me, and with a returned smile, she said, "Thank you!" I was relieved and I silently said to the Lord *Thank you, Lord for helping me to say the right thing to her.*

Back to College

S hortly after that, I went back to college and continued taking classes. When I got there, I got a job working third shift. This meant that I had to go visit the dean because I might not be able to attend the upcoming Bible conference.

When I went to the dean's office, I told him, "I have a job working third shift, so do I still have to attend the Bible conference?"

The dean asked me, "What hours are you working?"

"10 p.m. to 6 a.m."

He replied, "No, you don't have to go!"

"O.K., thank you!" I thought *I'll go anyway because I might learn something good.*

As I was attending, I found that I could only get about an hour rest before attending the conference. I found it hard to stay awake during the weeklong meeting.

One day at the conference, one of the speakers noticed that I was falling asleep in an audience of over 1,000 people. Looking right at me he said, "You! You need to pay attention to what I'm saying. I will not have people sleeping while I'm preaching! You need to stay awake!"

I looked around and I noticed that he must have been talking to me and my friend Mr. Pritchard nudged me and said, "I don't know you!"

So, I tried my best to stay awake for the conference for the rest of the week. My friend never sat next to me again after that happened, and I was not called out like that again in the conference. The Lord taught me more humility from this experience, which I always need. If I didn't humble my heart, I understand that God will do it for me to help me have a better prayer life. To have answers to prayer, I learned that I needed to repent first.

One of my favorite verses on prayer is Psalms 66:18, which says, "If I regard iniquity in my heart, the Lord will not hear me." (NKJV)

Matthew 6:33, "But seek ye first the kingdom of God and His righteousness, and all these things shall be added unto you." (NKJV)

It seems that whenever the Lord teaches me humility, He has a blessing He wants to give me. When someone curses me, or speaks ill of me, I say a polite "Thank you!" There have been a few times when the Lord blessed me monetarily as things like that happen.

A few days after, I was short on money, and it was time to do my laundry. My clothes really needed to be washed and it was a few more days before I got paid again from my job. I prayed and asked the Lord for two dollars so I could do my laundry.

Later that day, when I was walking down the street, a tall elderly black man approached and said to me, "Here's some money to help you with your needs."

"Thank you, sir!"

I believe that this man was most likely an angel of God, because only He knew of my need.

It was the two dollars that I had prayed for. I thought *If I had asked the Lord for more money maybe I would have gotten more!* Then I thought *Well, at least He did supply me with my need!*

I learned to accept gifts, even from strangers, because they come from God. If I don't accept the gift, I will rob both of us of a blessing.

Acts 20:35 says, "I have shown you in all things, how that so laboring you ought to support the weak, and to remember the words of the Lord Jesus, how he said, It is more blessed to give than to receive."

It was a small blessing, but it reminded me that God is always there, to help me no matter what I needed. If God wants to bless me with little things, then He can surely bless me with bigger ones.

This reminded me of Hebrews 13:5, "Let your conversation be without covetousness; and be content with such things as ye have: for he has said, I will never leave you nor forsake you." (KJV)

A Demonic Experience

I worked at the Y.W.C.O. (commonly referred to as the "Y") to help with my tuition and it was there that I encountered a woman who was demon possessed. They had rooms on the upper floors for transient women. Several of them came from a mental hospital when it was determined that they were ready to be on their own. The hospital treated the Y as if it were a halfway house for women. I was a desk clerk there and I met many of the women when they came down to the lobby where I worked.

There was one woman, who the other women said she was demon possessed. She sat down in the lobby near the elevators and stared in that direction away from me. Whenever I looked in her direction, she turned around and looked at me in fear. She did this three times and each time with the same fear in her eyes. Her head was facing away from me, so there was no way that she could see me when I looked at her.

I then knew that she was possessed, because there were no mirrors there, by which she could see me. I knew that demons fear Jesus, and I had Jesus in my heart. I also knew how to cast out demons and they probably knew it. James 2:19 says, "You believe that there is one God; you do well: the devils also believe and tremble." (KJV)

I thought about casting out the demon(s) from her but I was afraid of losing my job in the process. Also, she left the Y a short time later, so I had no way of seeing her again. I didn't know it at the time, but this would be my first of several encounters with demons.

A Divine Meeting

J im Marshall, a college friend of mine, had a girlfriend named Debbie. Jim was tall, so I always referred to him as "Big Jim."

One September day, Jim asked me, "We are trying to find a date for a friend of ours. Would you like to go on a date with her?"

He pointed to the lady that they were trying to hook me up with and I told him, "Thanks, but I'm already dating someone else."

Several days later, I met Jim and Debbie and their friend, Cindy, in the Happy Corner which was a snack bar at the college. I was there to buy my usual bag of peanuts and noticed their friend buying yogurt.

I approached them and said, "How are you doing big Jim?"

"I'm doing fine."

I sat down at a table that was a couple tables away from where they were sitting and Cindy told her friends, "I'm going to marry Terry someday."

They didn't believe her because she wouldn't even talk to me when we were in line buying our snacks.

Learning Humility Again

I found a school that wanted me to teach math and science. All I needed was to finish eight weeks of student teaching and then I could graduate. During that time, I found myself telling the lessons instead of teaching them. This meant that I wasn't making sure that the students were learning. I should have questioned the students, individually, about the material, to make sure they understood them. Because of that, they didn't seem to pay attention and didn't do so well on the quizzes and tests.

This looked bad on my part and I ended up not graduating. I believed that the problem was largely due to my stage fright that stemmed from my childhood. I was "knocked down" but not "knocked out." I didn't look at myself as a failure, as long as I endeavored to serve the Lord. Also, I didn't want to give up on teaching after all of those years at the university. Philippians 1:21says, "For me to live is Christ, and to die is gain." (KJV)

If I wanted to learn to swim, I had to jump into the pool. I just had to make sure that someone was there to pull me out if I started to drown. Just like Peter, I needed to have his boldness and take that step of faith, even if it was a little faith.

I prayed to the Lord and called a school that needed me to teach. The school wanted me to still come, even though I didn't finish my education. By God's grace, I went on to teach at a Christian school in Gastonia, North Carolina but found the first year to be quite difficult.

I noticed that my stage fright started to decline, so calling on individual students was easier. I was learning to overcome my bad thoughts about myself and the students seemed to be learning their lessons.

However, I ended up getting very little sleep at night because I was writing new lesson plans, grading papers, and coaching football or basketball after school. My health began to decline and my allergies began to really bother me. My allergies got so bad from not eating right that the students thought I was crying in the classroom.

I could have had the Director of Education come out to reevaluate me so that I could still graduate. The problem was that I had to pay for her to come out and pay for her hotel room. I didn't have that kind of money, and with all my problems, I didn't think that I had a chance. If I could borrow the money, I thought that it might possibly end up being a waste of time and expenses.

The school took my tithe out of my paycheck, so my paycheck was smaller. After the deduction, I was getting a salary that was equivalent to minimum wage. I was never a good tither, because I didn't believe in Old Testament tithing, but I did believe in New Testament giving. God has always blessed my giving and I've given more than just money. I wished that they would have included the money they took from me so that I could bless others. How could I give what I didn't have?

Since my teaching ability declined, I was asked to leave. I believed that the Lord was teaching me a lesson on humility by allowing these things to happen to me. (At least they didn't fire me.)

It didn't worry me at all, to know that I had to find another job, since I was getting such a small salary. I decided to check out another Baptist church nearby to see if I even wanted to stay in Gastonia. They were "too busy" for me to have a puppet ministry there, so I decided to go back to TriCity. I knew that I wouldn't have too much trouble finding a job back home.

I Peter 5:5 says, "…for God resists the proud, and gives grace to the humble." (KJV)

This grace is God's favor and love. I knew that God was going to bless me again, but I wanted Him to bless me so I could bless others.

A Classroom of Miracles

A t TriCity, in 1981, I was given the opportunity to teach a Sunday school class at the church. I really enjoyed teaching a class of seven-year-old boys and tried to do my best.

One Sunday, I was teaching about David and Goliath. I made a sling out of construction paper, string and an eraser for a rock. I told the class, "I'm going to show you just how easy it was for David to kill Goliath."

As I slung it around in circles, the boys all ducked under their desks and started laughing nervously. I'll admit I was a little nervous, too! When I released the eraser, it hit the chalk board on the other side of the room, behind the boys. With a big "WHACK," it hit right where I aimed it!

I looked and said, "Wow, I hope I didn't put a hole in the chalk board!" I looked closer at the board and saw that there was no damage. I was relieved!

On another Sunday, I talked about prayer.

"Today we are going to talk about how to pray and how God answers prayer. How many of you boys have had an answer to prayer?"

Some of the boys raised their hands, and then I said, "Today we are going to find out what our needs are and we are going to pray for them. I'm going to write them down in my notebook so that I won't forget them, and I won't let anyone know about it. We are only going to tell the <u>Lord</u> what our needs are, and I'm asking you to not tell anyone else, so that we can see the Lord does answer our prayers."

I then asked each of the ten boys, one by one, what they needed. Four boys said that they needed new shoes for school, three boys needed coats, one needed a bicycle so he could get to school and two of them needed prayers for their grandmothers' surgeries. I wrote all of these needs down, and then we prayed together for all of them.

A couple of weeks went by and we continued to talk about answers to prayer. By this time, nine of the boys all had their prayers answered except one who had been absent and out of town with his parents.

When he came back after four weeks, I asked him if his prayer was answered and he said, "My grandmother's surgery went O.K., and she is getting better." I was now excited that every boy in my class had an answer to prayer!

Matthew 6:31- 33, "Therefore do not worry, saying, 'What shall we eat?' or 'What shall we drink?' or 'What shall we wear?' For after these things the gentiles seek. For your heavenly Father knows that you need all these things. But seek first the kingdom of God and His righteousness, and all these things shall be added to you." (KNJV)

A Miracle Unfolding

I started praying more for the Lord to give me a wife. I noticed, in my church, that the young ladies were either married, engaged, or too young for me to date. I took this as an answer to my prayers, that God was saying "Not yet." So, I believed that God had a young lady for me somewhere else.

My mother told me that my second cousin, Tim and his wife Lisa were going to see his mother in Rocheport, Missouri. I determined to go visit them to have something to do, instead of moping around since I didn't have any good prospects for a wife. Tim was in the military and on leave, so he spent that time visiting his mother who was also my Great Aunt Edna.

When I arrived, we visited for a while talking about the military life and that Tim went to basic training in the army at Fort Leonard Wood. They told me that I should join the military. They also told me about the good pay and benefits that they were getting. Lisa told her mother-in-law and me that she was pregnant at the time and didn't know if it was a boy or a girl yet.

Edna said to Lisa, "I can tell if your baby is going to be a boy or a girl. I have a pendulum that I can wave over the baby. If the pendulum goes in circles, it will be a girl and if it swings back and forth it will be a boy"

She got out the pendulum and held it over where the baby was and shook it a little.

The pendulum began to go in circles, so Edna said, "It looks like you're going to have a girl!" (They did end up having a girl.)

This surprised me that she would do such a thing, being the Christian that I have always known her to be. I could remember visiting her church in New Franklin, several years ago, and she taught the class I was in.

For some reason, I felt compelled to say to Lisa, "Find me a wife."

She replied, "I have a sister who will be coming here in a couple weeks, she used to go to Tennessee Temple where you went to college and her name is Cindy Hauser!"

I gave her a picture of me to give to Cindy and said, "I'll be back in a couple of weeks to see her then!"

Lisa said to me, "I'll be sure to give it to her!"

"When was she at Tennessee Temple? I could look her up in my yearbook when I get back home!"

She replied, "Cindy was at Temple in 1978."

When I got home, I looked up her picture and noticed she was the young lady that was a friend of my friends, Jim and Debbie, who I met at Temple.

A Miracle Meeting

C indy got to Rocheport before I did and met with her sister Lisa and
Tim. Lisa said to her "Tim has a cousin named Terry Price who
wants to meet you tomorrow."

Cindy replied, "I just got out of a bad relationship, and I don't feel
like meeting anyone else right now!"

Lisa showed her the picture of me, and Cindy said with great surprise
that she would go ahead and meet me.

This surprised Lisa, too, that Cindy changed her mind so quickly.
Cindy told her, "We knew each other at Temple a few years ago, through
my friends Jim and Debbie."

I came the following day and met with all of them and we talked
about Tennessee Temple and how Lisa and Tim met each other. Cindy
and I had a good time talking about a lot of things, and she and I went
out to eat a pizza in nearby Booneville.

After I went back home, I continued to talk to her on the phone
and write her letters. Our relationship grew. I realized I wasn't making
much money if I was to get serious with Cindy, so I took on two jobs. I
had counted all of the girls that I had ever dated in my life and Cindy
was the 51st one.

On Valentine's Day of 1982, I proposed to her over the phone.

I asked her, "Will you marry me?"

She replied, "Yes."

Shortly after that, she came to visit me in Kansas City. When she arrived at the KCI airport, I put the engagement ring on her finger in the parking lot. While she stayed for a few days at my mother's friend's house, I took her around the city and to church.

After the visit, she went back home to Petersburg. I asked a friend of mine if there was a way to make extra money, because I was getting married. He told me that he donated plasma. My allergies didn't seem to bother me since I was eating healthier foods, so I started donating, too. (I needed this extra money to help with our honeymoon.)

A Wedding That Almost Wasn't

I left for Petersburg, Virginia, just days before the wedding and stopped by West Virginia to pick up David Farmer, a friend of mine that I met at TriCity. I introduced him to everyone and told them that he would be the Best Man at the wedding.

After that, the first thing he said was, "Let's go to the beach and check out the girls."

Several of us heard him say that and the comment made Cindy's mother and grandmother very upset that he would say such a thing.

When David realized what he did was wrong, he said, "I was just joking."

My soon to be mother-in-law said to me, "David will have to leave, we can't have him in the wedding."

Apparently, they didn't believe him and Cindy's grandparents sent him back to his home with some travel money. I have never known him to tell a lie, but I thought it might be hard to convince them, because they just met him. From that experience, I learned to never joke around people unless they got to know me well, first.

I never saw David again after that, but a friend told me he died from a bad heart some years later. He needed surgery on his heart, which seemingly, he never could afford.

Cindy said, "We'll have to cancel the wedding."

I replied, "Let's see if we can work something out so that we can still have the wedding."

"What can we do?"

"Maybe, we could get Jeff to be the Best Man! He's about the same size as David."

Jeff was the youth director at Cindy's church and to our surprise, when he tried on the tuxedo, it fit him perfectly. He agreed to be the Best Man, so the wedding was on again.

I wore a white tuxedo and Cindy wore a white wedding dress that she had made. I wore white to represent the fact that I was a virgin. The wedding party wore purple and white since purple was her favorite color.

As the wedding progressed, a big flying bug that looked like a beetle flew in and landed on Cindy, which caused a lot of laughter as many people saw it, too.

After that, I thought to myself *What could happen next?*

A lady named Myra sang "The Lord's Prayer." Right after that, the candles that were lit, melted down enough to catch a hanging paper streamer on fire. A couple of men ran forward to put out the fire and the guests laughed nervously. The ceremony continued without any further incidents and we were married on June 18, 1982. This happened to be the same day of the year when my parents were married. It was the third most important decision in my life.

We didn't have much money at the time, but we gave the most valuable gift a person could give to their spouse and that was our virginity. I was 27 years old and she was 22.

We earlier had decided to take my car to church and leave her car home. We knew that they would decorate mine, so we took her car to go on our honeymoon.

God Protected Our Honeymoon

B efore we left for our honeymoon, I prayed, "Please Lord give us a safe trip and watch over us and protect us."

We went to Washington, D.C. and visited several places. One place we went to was the Washington Monument. We took the elevator to the top and could see for miles around and got acquainted with the layout of the area. It was an enjoyable view.

When we got back to our hotel, we watched the news. The newsman said, "There was a robbery in the Washington Monument by a gunman who robbed everyone in the elevator around noon, today."

I said to Cindy, "It was around 11:30 when we were there, so it must have happened with the next group that went up."

I was thankful that it didn't happen to us but felt sorry for those who were robbed. I remember seeing the people who were next to get on the elevator. They all looked like they were going to have a nice time. The Lord was looking out for us that day, and thankfully, He answered my prayer.

Amos 3:10, "For they do not know to do right, says the Lord, who store up violence and robbery in their palaces." (NKJV) It's never right to do wrong!

We first lived in Petersburg, Virginia, and our address was box 17H. I didn't know this at the time, but the number 17 in our address would be repeated several more times as we moved from place to place. We first lived in a double-wide mobile home that Cindy's family had lived in.

Cindy's Car Miracles

I made it a habit to pray for Cindy like this: "Dear Father in heaven, forgive me of my sins. I pray that you would watch over Cindy and bring her home safely from work."

One rainy day, she was driving her Honda Civic home from work. She took a curve too fast and the car flipped in the air. Miraculously, it landed on all four tires on the side of the road. She was able to maintain control and drive it home without any damage to the car.

When she got home and told me about it, I had to see for myself. I looked all around the car and couldn't find any damage.

Another time she drove home from work, she was in an accident, around 5:30 p.m., when someone rear-ended her. The ambulance came and had to remove a rod from her leg to get her out. I was still in bed because I worked third shift. At the exact same time of her accident, I heard three knocks on the bedroom door. There was no one else at home. I believe that it was one of God's angels that I heard knocking.

I thought it was really unusual to hear knocks on that door, so I answered back, "Who's there?"

With no answer, I said it again louder, "Who's there?"

When I still heard no reply, I realized that something may have happened to Cindy, because she was usually on her way home at that time of the day.

I prayed, "Lord please help Cindy if something has happened to her. Please keep her safe and bring her home soon."

About an hour after I prayed, I got a phone call from Cindy.

"Terry, I'm at the Petersburg Hospital. I was in an accident with my car. They finished bandaging my leg, because a rod went into it. I'm alright now and you can come to pick me up. And guess what? They found out that I'm pregnant!"

I felt really bad about Cindy's accident, but at least she was able to recover from it. At the same time, I was glad to know that we were going to have a baby.

These mixed emotions reminded me of Romans 8:28, "And we know that all things work together for good to those who love God, to those who are the called according to His purpose." (NKJV)

Debra was born on June 7, 1983, at the same hospital where Cindy and her mother were born. I look at any birth as being a miracle because it's at conception that God creates the soul.

Psalms 139:14 -16, "I will praise You, for I am fearfully and wonderfully made; Marvelous are Your works, and that my soul knows very well. My frame is not hidden from You, when I was made in secret, and skillfully wrought in the lowest parts of the earth. Your eyes saw my substance being yet unformed. And in Your book, they are written…" (NKJV)

Cindy kept telling me that there were ghosts in our house. A few years before, her family was playing with a Ouija Board and they had been having problems since then. It didn't help that the mobile home sat next to a Civil War trench. Most often she saw a Civil War soldier standing in the doorway of our bedroom. I believed her, but they didn't bother me, so I let it go on for a while to see if anything else would happen.

One night, when something grabbed my toes while I was lying in bed, I then decided to do something about it. I had been listening to cassette tapes that taught about demonology and used what I had learned to get rid of the demons. I told the demons to leave in the name of Jesus and they did. We didn't seem to have any more problems after that, but I kept saying that prayer for several nights just to be safe.

Moving to Columbia, Missouri

Since we weren't making enough money where we were living, and we had a new baby girl that we had to take care of, we decided to move to Columbia, Missouri. I wanted to see if I could work in the prison that my Uncle Carroll told Mom about. I thought I might have a chance since he could help me. He had a son-in-law, Tom Clements, who was already working in a Missouri prison.

We were able to purchase a mobile home, but the trailer park was full. There was someone moving out in 45 days, so we decided to move onto their lot. I prayed and asked God to help us find a place to temporarily live. The Lord led us to a friend who offered to let us move our mobile home onto his property until the lot was open. His address was box 17, so I believed it was God's will for us to be there.

When we were able to move our trailer into the trailer park, they told us that lot 17 was the one that was available. With that in mind, we knew it was God's will again.

I didn't get the job working at the prison. A security job I had didn't work out for me financially, so I ended up working at the University of Missouri, Columbia. I prayed and asked the Lord to help me find a good job. The Lord reminded me of my cousin, Tim, who was still doing well financially, in the military, so it encouraged me to join. When I told my boss I was going to join the Army and was preparing to go, Cindy was able to get a job at UMC, too.

God's Protection in the Army

I went to Fort Benning, Georgia, on October 25, 1984 and found training was pretty tough but I managed to make it in the infantry without too much trouble. I had to go through eight weeks of basic and five weeks of advanced infantry training. By God's grace, it was only a few times I ran into difficulties.

During the time I was in basic, we did some pugil stick training. I got hit in the chest several times when I had to fight with two other soldiers at the same time. This caused me to have chest pains that would last with me throughout my Army career. The doctors called my condition "costochondritis."

When I was in advanced training at Fort Benning, Georgia, I had a unique experience while on a ten mile road march. We had to do a quick march and we had to finish it within two hours.

About three miles into the march, I felt something hit me very hard in my stomach and when I looked down, I saw an eight-point mule deer flash before me. I was in a lot of pain and fortunately not from a flesh wound or broken ribs, but the deer hit me hard enough to knock the wind out of me. I believe that it was a miracle that I didn't get gored because he must have turned his head away from me before the impact.

The drill sergeants noticed my encounter and could not help but laugh at me and my excruciating pain. When they saw I was all bent over trying to catch my breath, they had me march in the middle of the road so they could watch me because I was unable to march like the others. After a few miles, I caught my breath and finished with the others. The men in my company started calling me "The deer hunter," because of the recent movie called "The Dear Hunter." I can laugh about this now, but I sure couldn't then!

One thing I did know, was, I always prayed every day and that God had protected me from possible death. I thanked the Lord that I made the road march.

One of the last things I had to do to pass basic was to do the two mile run. I had finished it before in the required time for my age, so I felt I could do well this last time.

I was doing fine in the run until I came around the last turn on the track. My left arch fell when I heard a pop in my foot. I had about 60 yards to go and all I could do was limp my way to the finish line. Thankfully, I finished with a qualifying time.

I managed to make it through all my training and got orders to go to my first duty station at Ft. Benning with the 197th Mechanized Infantry. Cindy found an apartment in Columbus, Georgia, that we moved to and it happened to be apartment 17C.

I asked her, "How did we end up with another '17'?"

She assured me, "It was the only two-bedroom apartment that was available."

"O.K. it must be God's will for us to live there!"

A Tour in Hawaii

I filled out a dream list of the places that I would like to be stationed at in the Army when my tour was about up in Georgia. At the top of the list, I put Hawaii. Somehow, I managed to get orders to go there after a lot of praying. This happened to be Cindy's dream, too. She had traveled in her life to every state except Alaska and Hawaii.

While stationed in Hawaii, two more miracles were born in Tripler Army Hospital. Donald (Donny) was born on November 4, 1986, and Jonathan (Jon) was born on December 31, 1987. Donny, born with blonde hair and blue eyes, was one who enjoyed the attention that we gave him. Jon, being cute as a baby, seemed to enjoy life and to be held.

We didn't live at an address with the number 17 in Hawaii, except when you add up the numbers in the address; 4904C (4 + 9 + 0 + 4 = 17.) We got to live on post after a few months after living in Mililani Town. Our home was only two miles from where I worked so I rode my bike to there every day to get more exercise.

While I was working, Cindy took our three kids to the beaches and other places around the island of Oahu. She also had a distant relative that she met at church and they went island hopping together. One time they took a cheap military flight to Los Angeles and ate at a restaurant there.

My unit went to places like Thailand and the Big Island of Hawaii for training. There were some mountains on our island of Oahu called the Kahukus that was also used for military training.

One time when we were training in the Kahukus, we did a hard march. We were marching up and down mountain ridges during the night for several hours, and I was carrying a lot of rounds for an M60 machinegun. They began to feel very heavy after carrying them for so long. It was around 3 a.m. when I stepped into a ditch and twisted my ankle under all of that weight.

Right at that time, Cindy heard three knocks on our bedroom door. She remembered the knocks that happened before when we lived in Petersburg, so she knew that there was something wrong with me and she prayed for me. A military ambulance came and bandaged up my ankle. I was put on light duty and it ended up being about three weeks for my ankle to completely heal.

The Miracle That Might
Have Happened

W e had a training exercise that I went to at Camp Friendship in Thailand for four weeks. This had been a staging area during the Viet Nam War.

When we finished our training, we boarded a C-5 plane which was very large with four big engines. It was big enough inside the belly of the plane to have helicopters and tanks anchored down inside it. As we flew home from there, all we could see was water down below, no land anywhere and very few clouds.

We were about a few hours on our flight and then we heard the navigator say in a calm voice, "Attention, attention, everyone! We have something wrong with one of our engines. We don't know what it is, but there is something wrong."

Immediately, there was silence in the plane. I turned around in my seat to see why they were so quiet and it looked like they were all in silent prayer. I made my prayer a quick one, only because I remembered praying before we boarded. Our plane did go down, but we managed to land on an atoll in the South Pacific.

When the plane first touched the runway, it bounced back up. Everyone started cheering right after the wheels touched. They touched the runway again after a few seconds and as the plane stayed on the runway everyone started clapping.

We had to stay there for a few hours until they had another plane ready. Many of the soldier's wives kept coming to the barracks every day to find out any news of when their husbands were coming home.

Word got back to the barracks, concerning the plane, and the Staff Duty Sergeant said that the plane went down as it was going over the Pacific Ocean. He was only partly right, but until the message was corrected, the wives were in a lot of panic.

I don't know for sure if a miracle happened that day. At least our prayers could have made things better than what could have happened if we didn't pray. I believe that it's "better to be safe than sorry." To me, it was a miracle to see so many in prayer.

We should have the attitude, no matter the altitude, to always pray for each other.

Ephesians 6:18 reads, "Praying always with all prayer and supplication in the Spirit, being watchful to this end with all perseverance and supplication for all the saints." (NKJV)

Trusting in the Lord

After much prayer, I reenlisted in the Army, and shortly after that, I received orders to move to Fort Bragg, North Carolina, Jeremy was born on May 17, 1991, at Womack Army Hospital. As a child, he was really smart and learned things quickly.

He would be the last of our miracle children because we couldn't afford to have any more. The army paid for our three boys, which saved us thousands of dollars.

One day, when I was out in the field training with my unit, the zipper got stuck in my sleeping bag. It had a hood on it so I wasn't able to slide out of it. I felt like I was in a cocoon. I noticed I was starting to panic due to fear of being stuck for a long time. I called out to my Sergeant who was near me and told him my zipper was stuck. I asked him if he could get me out. He got out a knife and started working on the zipper.

I prayed and asked the Lord, "Please Jesus, help me to get out of this sleeping bag."

I found myself to be less panicked and my heart beat slowed down. I remembered the verses in the Bible that said:

Trust in the Lord with all your heart and

Lean not unto your own understanding

In all your ways acknowledge Him and

He will make your paths straight (NKJV)

(The underlined letters spell "**H.I.L.T.**" backward which means "thoroughly" or "completely" and this is the way I try to follow the Lord.)

I put my trust in Jesus by believing He would help me. I put out the thought that I was going to be stuck for a long time and thought only about Him and the verse. It only took my Sergeant about two minutes to break the zipper free, but it seemed much longer.

Months before my reenlistment was up, the government was doing a draw-down of the military. They offered early out bonuses, so I prayed to the Lord about it. I felt impressed to go ahead and get out because they offered a big bonus. My health was making it difficult to stay in and I felt there was no chance I could stay. I was still having allergy problems and pain in my chest from the pugil stick training. Because of my injuries, a promotion was not an option.

Days before I got out, they kept messing up my paperwork. After the third time, they finally got it right after much prayer. I believed that the Devil didn't want me to get out with that much money.

With everything included, I ended up with more than $16,000. After we completely paid off our bills, we bought some needed furniture. We had enough money to carry us for the next three months.

When I realized that good jobs were hard to find in a military town like Fayetteville, I looked in the newspaper for jobs. The paper said that the best jobs were in the Dallas/Fort Worth area in Texas. I knew that my brother, Tony, lived in The Colony, just north of Dallas. So, I moved in with him until I could find a job. Uncle Carroll also happened to live in the area, doing construction work.

Once a job was found, I had Cindy and the children move to Texas. Cindy and I went to a mobile home dealer to buy a home.

The lady who sold us the home asked, "Are you Christians?"

We both replied, "Yes."

I thought *She must be a devout Christian if she is asking a question like that.*

We bought the home and had it moved to a trailer park in Lewisville to lot 17. As time went by, we noticed that the trailer was haunted. My sons would tell me about a lady pushing a stroller in their bedroom. Jeremy said that he was talking to a little girl named Ashley, too.

I realized that the home was definitely haunted, so I went around to each room and prayed "Lord, please forgive me of my sins. I claim the Blood of Jesus, please remove these demons from this room and from our home, in Jesus' Name, Amen."

The demons were gone after that, and I could feel the peace that was in the home. The children made no more complaints about the things that they saw or heard. Cindy went to the people who sold us the mobile home. They told her that a man had killed his wife, two children, and then himself in the home.

Cindy told them that Jeremy was talking to Ashley. They were shocked that Cindy somehow knew the girl's name that was killed there.

So, in spite of the problems that we had there, Cindy and I knew it was God's will to stay.

A Miracle that Didn't Happen

After living there for several months, Cindy chose numbers for the lottery, around May of 1993. The numbers were the same as the ages of all six of us in our family. She showed me the numbers and said she was going to play them.

Days before, I received a letter from a psychic telling us that we would be lottery winners soon and to respond back to her quickly with a small payment.

I told Cindy, "I got a letter from a psychic a few days ago, stating that we were going to win the lottery. She was going to help us if we paid her some money."

Cindy replied, "I don't want anything to do with psychics."

Her reply convinced me that much more to not play the lottery. I was in a hurry to get to work, and Cindy ended up being too tired to go play the numbers.

It so happened that if she or I played those numbers, we would have won $4,000,000. Actually, I'm glad that we didn't because people might find that we took advice from a psychic. This would have been a bad testimony of Christian faith. I felt that my reputation was worth more than all that money.

Ecclesiastes 10:1, says, "Dead flies putrefy the perfumer's ointment, and cause it to give off a foul odor; so does a little folly to one respected for wisdom and honor." (NKJV)

Also, I was concerned that we would end up relying less on the Lord. If we had all this money, then we might not pray as much for God's help. I was afraid it might even hurt our marriage as it has done to others who played the lottery.

I Timothy 6:9 says, "But those who desire to be rich fall into temptation and a snare, and into many foolish and harmful lusts which drown men in destruction and perdition." (NKJV)

A Miracle in Jackson, Tennessee

C indy and I saved enough money to take a two-week vacation at Christmas time. We were able to take our vacations at the same time and the children were out of school. We decided to go visit Cindy's Mom in Georgia for the duration.

We were aware of the bad weather that we might have on our trip, but we believed it would stay north of us. We made it all the way to Tennessee without any problems. When we got there, I saw a sign that indicated how many miles it was to Jackson.

It reminded me of Johnny Cash's song "Jackson" and started singing it in my mind, in my own way: *I'm going to Jackson, Jackson, Tennessee; I'm going to Jackson, Jackson Tennessee.*

I didn't realize it at the time but the thought would be prophetic. The temperature had dropped below freezing and roads were beginning to ice. As we were traveling on Interstate 40, I saw ahead of us, what looked like solid ice and I noticed that she was doing about 50.

With certainty in my voice, I said, "You need to slow down, you're going too fast!"

As soon as she started slowing down, she hit the ice. The car started sliding straight towards a guard rail where the Interstate curved to the left.

I quickly told everyone, "Hang on tight, we're about to crash!"

As we were just seconds away from hitting the rail, I prayed aloud that no one would be hurt. We didn't spin around because if we did, there would have been a lot more damage.

We went up the inclined part of the rail and left the right side suspended about a foot in the air. We could've crashed into the side of the railing and had a lot more damage and possible injuries, but I believe that the Lord protected us.

I turned around, looking at everyone and said, "Is everyone alright?"

Debra said, "We're all O.K., but Donny got a bump on his head, so God didn't answer your prayer, Dad!"

"I believe He did because things could have been a lot worse."

It was a relief to know Donny's small bump on his head wasn't bad enough to take him to the hospital.

When I climbed out of the car, I noticed that the rail split open our gas tank. I told everyone to get out and a few minutes later a wrecker truck came by to help us. He was able to free the car from the rail, but he bent the right rear axle in the process.

He took the car to a repair shop about two miles back and the mechanic said they could fix it the next day. There was a motel within walking distance so we spent the night there.

The following morning, we went to the shop and they told us how much it would be to replace the tank and that they could bend the axle back. I was relieved that it didn't cost us more money than what we had.

I said to the mechanic, "I'm surprised that our gas tank didn't catch on fire."

He replied, "It would have been a lot worse if it was a full tank."

"Then I'm glad that it was only about half full!"

I figured that the ice on the rail might have prevented it, plus my prayer.

The lady at the desk said, "We pray every morning that people who travel through here will have safe trips."

I replied, "Thank you!"

I believed their prayers helped us, too!

After the car was fixed, I asked the mechanic, "Do you think that the road is clear enough to keep going east?"

"The roads are still all ice further east of here."

A reporter from the local newspaper came by and said to us, "I'm doing a report on the road conditions and the accidents, so I'd like to take you all to a restaurant and ask you some questions."

There was a restaurant within a short walk of the motel. When we met the reporter, she asked us a few questions and paid for our meal.

After meeting with her, Cindy said in an asserted voice, "We don't have enough money left to make it back home after paying for the repairs."

I replied, "We could go visit my mom in Missouri because the roads were clear in her direction and closer than going back home."

Cindy said, "I can call Mom and see if she could send us some money. If she can't, we'll just have to drive back home."

I prayed about it and said, "She could send the money to my mom's house and we could cash it there."

Cindy's mother sent us the money when we got to Missouri, so we were able to take a full vacation.

Matthew 17:20 reads, "And Jesus said unto them, Because of your unbelief: for verily I say to you, If you have faith as a grain of mustard seed, you shall say to this mountain. Remove hence from yonder place; and it shall remove; and nothing shall be impossible to you." (KJV)

I didn't believe it took a lot of faith or a long prayer to make this happen. I also believed that even though Donny did get a little hurt, my prayer kept him from serious injury.

Donny's Miracle

I was teaching my son, Donny, about God answering prayer and told him how God answered some of mine. We were out of milk and couldn't buy any until next payday. So, Donny asked the Lord to give him some milk since he really liked it.

Within two hours, a boy who lived near us came knocking on our door. When Donny opened the door, he saw him holding a gallon of milk. He said that they were moving and they couldn't take the milk with them or it would go bad. He took the milk, thanked him, and told us what happened. I was glad to see that God answered his prayer and it did seem to strengthen his faith.

Matthew 7:7, "Ask and it will be given to you; seek and you shall find; knock, and it will be opened to you." (NKJV)

A Small Miracle

W e didn't have a lot of money, because our jobs in security didn't pay well, but we always seemed to make ends meet. We came to a point where we needed over $600 because of pressing bills. I got on my knees and prayed the Lord's Prayer and then asked that the Lord would give us the money to get caught up on our debt.

Within a few days, I received a savings bond in the mail from my step-grandmother, Marie. I prayed "Thank you, Lord for answering my prayer and giving me just what I needed." After paying our bills, we had about four dollars left over. Ephesians 2:20 says, "Now to Him who is able to do exceedingly abundantly above all that we ask or think, according to the power that works in us." (NKJV)

A Miracle Cure and Another 17

C indy struggled with depression most of her life. I prayed she would be able to get over it so she could handle life better, because her depression worsened and affected all of us.

I wrote her a country song titled "Don't mount Up Your Horse" that I hoped would help because her problem seemed to even hurt our relationship. She discovered country music seemed to make things worse, so this song didn't help her at all. I should have chosen something other than the country music style.

Cindy's depression started to go away when she quit listening to that kind of music. She started focusing on listening to Christian music, instead and it helped.

After living in Lewisville, we decided to move to Valley View, Texas. We thought it would be best for our children to have their own bedrooms since they were growing older.

When we bought the land and the mobile home, I added up all of the numbers in our address, it came out to 102. I divided that number by 17 and came up with "6." (6x17=102.) Because of this, we knew by this that it was God's will for us to live there.

The Sign Again

O ne day, when I turned on the TV, I happened to watch a talk show I never had seen before.

The host asked the guest, "What is the most unusual floating debris that has ever been found?"

This question caught my attention because of the sign at the beach I found when I was a child.

The guest answered, "There was a sign that floated from Egypt to Southern California that said 'Port Said' on it. It's now in a museum in Southern California."

This surprised me in such a way that it felt like I was dreaming. They were talking about the same sign that I had found all those years ago. I knew where it was now. I believe the Lord wanted me to see this show. It was also God's perfect timing to turn on the television.

It seemed like the Lord was saying to me, "Terry, I love you and you know that all things belong to me. Thank you for finding my sign. Because of what you did, it is now safe in a museum."

The Lord made peace with me and I with Him.

James 3:17-18, "But the wisdom that is from above is first pure, then peaceable, gentle, willing to yield, full of mercy and good fruits, without partiality and without hypocrisy. Now the fruit of righteousness is sown in peace by those who make peace" (NKJV)

The Psychic's Sign

I drove by a psychic's office every day I went to work. One day, the Lord laid it upon my heart to pray that the sign, in front of the office, would come down, so I prayed, "Lord please forgive me of my sins and take the psychic's sign down. I claim the blood of Jesus and keep the demons away from the psychic. In Jesus' name, amen."

I did this for several months. One day, as I drove to work about an hour before sunrise, I saw a fire truck in front of the building. The office was burning down and I felt bad that it did.

About two weeks later, after the fire, the sign was taken down. I told my pastor, about my prayer.

He smiled and said, "It looks like that psychic didn't see what was coming."

"I have been praying for that psychic for several months before it all happened."

"I'm sure that there were other people who were praying like you did, too."

I'm sure that he was right because there are many Christians who pray for many things and even things of that nature.

While I was at his church in Sanger, Texas, I did several puppet plays and one of the funniest was a play called "Miracles." I also took time to write poems.

The Eighth 17 Miracle

I was 51 when we started looking for another home, in Sanger. We found a community that looked really nice to us. We went to the realtor who had an office in a model home and talked to her. She showed us a map of all of the available lots in the developing neighborhood.

Cindy looked at the map that was color coded to show the number of bedrooms of each home and which were available. We were looking for a four-bedroom home that we could afford. She noticed that there was only one that was recently built that fit our needs. It happened to be on lot 17.

Cindy pointed to the map and said, "That's the one we want and I know that it's the one for us."

The lady replied, "Why do you say that?"

I said, "We have lived in several homes in our past that had either "lot 17" on it or "17" in the house address. So, I had faith that this is the one for us, too."

It ended up, after our talk and a lot of praying, we were able to buy the house, which was big enough for our family. After staying there for 5 years, we bought a mobile home after our children grew up and moved out of our house.

This totals up to 6 addresses with the actual 17 in them and two that had numbers adding up to 17! How can anyone figure the probability of something like this happening? I see it as a miracle, because, only God could have done something like this.

I believe that He was showing me that He is with us wherever we go. God is a sovereign God and can do anything He wants. To top it all off, since Cindy and I have been married, we lived in 17 different places from Petersburg to Sanger. Will Sanger be the last of the 17s? Only the Lord knows!

Here is a summary of all of the places we lived:

> Virginia = 1 (Box 17H, Petersburg)
>
> Missouri = 3 (South Columbia; Box 17, Hallsville; Lot 17, North Columbia)
>
> Georgia = 4 (Ft. Bragg; Apt. 17C, Columbus; two trailers in Columbus)
>
> Hawaii = 3 (Aiea; Mililani Town; 4904C, Schofield Barracks)
>
> North Carolina = 1 (Fayetteville)
>
> Texas = 5 (Carrollton; Lot 17, Lewisville; 53 on lot 49, Valley View; East Sanger; lot 17,
>
> TOTAL = 17

I also believe that sometimes the Lord puts numbers in our lives to remind us of what a mighty God we serve. He's constantly there for us whenever we need Him.

God knows every decision that I make, whether it is good or bad. What I do today has an effect on my future and the way God will bless me with miracles. So, if I want miracles to happen in my life, I need to start making it my goal to serve the Lord every day!

Philippians 3:13, 14 says, "Brethren, I do not count myself to have apprehended: but one thing I do, forgetting those things which are behind and reaching forward to the things which are ahead. I press toward the goal for the prize of the upward call of God in Christ Jesus." (NKJV)

An Unexpected Miracle

I decided to ask the Lord to give me $10,000 to help us to get out of debt. We never got that amount all at once. God helped us to get extra money in other ways by providing our needs as they came along.

Whenever our cars broke down, we seemed to have the money beforehand to pay for repairs. It was usually just the right amount to pay that bill or repair we needed. The Lord has provided us with much more money than I prayed for. We even managed to get raises at work.

Whenever we got extra money, I thought *We better hang on to this money for emergencies.* It happened a few times that way and I was glad I hung on to the money instead of buying things we really didn't need.

Matt. 6:8, "Therefore do not be like them. For your Father knows the things you have need of before you ask Him." (NKJV)

The Wobbly Wheel

O ne day, we noticed one of the wheels on Cindy's car was starting to wobble.

I said to her, "You need to get that wheel fixed before it comes off. I don't want you to be in a bad accident."

"I have to get to work and don't have time to fix it. I'll get it fixed on my way home when I stop by Pep Boys in Denton."

"I wish that you could stop there on your way to work."

"I can't lose any hours at work right now."

"OK, I'll be praying for you to have a safe trip to work and back to Denton. Call me when you get to work, so I know that you got there safely."

"Alright, she said, "I'll be praying, too!"

She drove to work safely and called me to let me know. Next, all I had to do was to pray that she would make it safely to Pep Boys.

She made it to the repair shop after work, called me and said, "Terry, I made it to Pep Boys."

"Good! I'm really glad you made it there! Are you OK?"

"Yes, I'm OK, but when they put the car up on the lift, the wheel fell off and hit the mechanic on the foot."

The car was repaired and she was able to drive safely home from the shop. I was relieved to know nothing bad had happened to her and nothing else was wrong with the car.

I believe the Lord had this planned to test our faith. It could have been a very dangerous situation, but the Lord protected her and I thanked the Him for it.

Psalms 91:11-12 says, "For He shall give His angels charge over you, to keep you in your ways. In their hands, they shall bear you up, least you dash your foot against a stone." (NKJV)

I had faith the Lord preserved her life because He isn't finished with her yet. He has great plans for her life.

Philippians 1:6 says, "being confident of this very thing, that He who has begun a good work in you will complete it until the day of Jesus Christ." (NKJV)

A Letter to a Psychic

I received a letter in the mail from another psychic. She said she was a Christian medium and could help me with my luck. She gave me some lucky numbers and included a form to fill out to return with some money.

I decided to write back to her and tell her about I John 4:1-4. I wrote it by hand because I felt she would be more likely to read it if I did.

"Beloved, do not believe every spirit, but test the spirits, whether they are of God; because many false prophets have gone out into the world."

"By this you know the Spirit of God: Every spirit that confesses that Jesus Christ has come in the flesh is of God,"

"and every spirit that does not confess that Jesus has come in the flesh is not of God. And this is the spirit of the Antichrist which you have heard is coming, and now already is in the world."

"You are of God, little children, and have overcome them, because He who is in you is greater that he who is in the world." (NKJV)

I prayed for a few days that the psychic would read my letter and get saved. I also prayed for God's protection from any demons that might come our way.

Five days after I sent the letter, I saw two shadowy figures come out of the ground near a house I was driving by at 10:00 pm. They looked a lot like shadows of the cartoon character Gumby, but with straight arms and legs. They brought no harm to me, but it did appear that they stared at me.

At the very same time, Cindy was awakened by several voices in the room. They seemed to be arguing with each other, but they didn't harm Cindy, either.

Ephesians 6:11 says, "Put on the whole armor of God, that you may be able to stand against the wiles of the devil." (NKJV)

Cindy and Her "Grandfather"

N ot too long after that, Cindy had to deal with the wiles of the devil. These wiles happened to her when she was visited by a demon who posed as her grandfather.

When she told me about her Grandfather, I told her to test this spirit by asking him if he believed that Jesus came in the flesh. So, the next time he came, she asked him and he gave her no answer. She then asked him to leave and he never came back, again.

It was interesting that I was in a deep sleep whenever her "grandfather" appeared. This convinced me more that she was talking to a demon.

I have learned that when we die, we go to be with the Lord. There is no lingering around after we die to take care of any unfinished business before we meet Him.

II Corinthians 5:8 says, "We are confident, yes well pleased rather to be absent from the body and to be present with the Lord." (NKJV)

God's Revenge

I worked in a warehouse in the Fort Worth area as a security officer. One of the other officers decided to write a false report against me so she could have a friend of hers take my place. I wrote a rebuttal on the back of the report that should have vindicated me, but our supervisor took her word for it, instead. I was pulled off of the post as a result.

Many months later, she showed up looking for a job where Cindy was a manager looking for guards to work at her warehouse. She saw Cindy's name tag and asked if she and I were related. Cindy told her that we were and she walked away without trying to apply.

We learned to not take revenge on others when they do wrong. Rather, we let the Lord have His revenge, because He can do a much better job than we can.

Deuteronomy 32:35 says, "Vengeance is Mine, and recompense; their foot shall slip in due time; for the day of their calamity is at hand, and the things to come hasten upon them." (NKJV)

Demons at Work

I worked in security with a friend and we both worked the same hours on a post. He worked three different jobs and saved up a lot of money to send his wife to Mexico to visit relatives for a couple of months.

While she was there, her stepbrother was practicing voo doo. Unfortunately, she got involved in it, too. My friend started seeing ghosts where we worked, while she was away. I told him that they were demons impersonating people.

I also saw a demon at our post. It looked like a skinny representation of the cartoon character, Casper the Friendly Ghost. He was looking in our window from the outside with his right hand above his eyes as if it improved his ability to look at me.

My friend said to me, "My wife came back from Mexico and gave me a charm. She told me if I wear it, it will give me good luck and keep evil away"

I replied to him, "Whatever you do, don't wear it! It will do the opposite of what she told you. That is how they bring demons to you, and you will start having bad things happen to you."

"OK, I will give it back to her and tell her what you said."

When he got home, he started seeing demons, there, too.

The next day at work, my friend told me, "I'm having problems with demons in our home."

"It's probably because of your wife's stepbrother bringing them to you."

"I tried to pray them away, and they wouldn't leave."

"I can pray the demons away. I've had several experiences with them in my past and have gotten rid of them before, so I'll help you with that."

I started praying for him every day, but after a couple of weeks I forgot to pray for him on the weekend.

He came back the following Monday and told me, "I saw demons over the weekend."

I told him, "I'm sorry. I forgot to pray for you over the weekend. I will remember to do it from now on until we can get rid of them completely. Only born-again Christians can keep them away by prayer. If you were a born-again Christian, you could do the same thing. To be a born-again Christian, you have to repent of your sins and ask Jesus into your heart. You can do it right now if you like"

He replied, "I don't want to do it right now."

I assumed he meant he would do it when he got home.

The next day, he said to me, "I'm not having any problems with demons anymore, I prayed them away."

From what he told me, I believed that he, too, was a born-again Christian.

Demons have some power that God has allowed them. They can cause miracles to happen, but they can't create something from nothing and they can't destroy souls. To get rid of demons is a miracle, itself.

Matthew 10:28, "And do not fear those who kill the body but cannot kill the soul. But rather fear Him who is able to destroy both soul and body in hell." (NKJV)

John 1:12 says, "But as many as received Him, to them He gave the right to become children of God, to those who believe in His name." (NKJV)

Bringing T.J. back to the Lord

My brother, T.J., was a free-lance comedy writer for some family oriented radio stations. He was always careful about his language he used because of his convictions. He was well liked and well known for his comedy that he both wrote and performed. I thought he was a little risqué at times, but he was funny.

For several years after our parents divorced, I prayed for T.J. that he would come back to serving the Lord. I'm sure that others prayed for him, too. He started to change his life when he found out that he had cancer.

It was first in his elbow and after the cancer was removed, it looked like it wasn't coming back. He got involved in a good church in Kansas City and started a class where he studied a men's ministry workbook.

A short time after that, he went back to the doctor and found that he had cancer in his kidney. He had the kidney removed and later found that it had spread to other parts of his body. He knew that he was dying and had a short time to live, so he determined to do a few things before he died.

One thing he wanted to do was to finish his workbook which took a few months to complete. He also was able to lead his son Patrick to the Lord and attend his wedding.

The last thing he was able to do was to make it to his 50th birthday. His birthday was August 7th, 1963 and he died August 20th, 2013.

I think that if T.J. had a life verse, it would be Philippians 3:13, 14.

Plasma Donations

I have donated plasma at different plasma centers off and on whenever I could, from 1982 to 2001, as we moved. I don't know how many donations I had made during those years, but I suppose it was from 50 to 100.

When we moved to Texas, I began to donate more frequently. For about two years from 1999 to 2001, I donated in Grand Prairie, Texas. They didn't keep a record of how much plasma I donated, (at least to my knowledge) so I quit going there. Then I decided to start donating in Denton, Texas from 2001 to 2015, because it was closer to where I lived, and they kept good records.

By May 11, 2015, after 13½ years, I managed to donate 894.206 liters of plasma. (This is equivalent to about 340 gallons.) I sent in the required paperwork to Guinness World Records and was accepted. (Since then, I donated a little more, which is unofficially about 920 liters total.) I am listed under "Most Blood Donated- Apheresis" as of this day.

I couldn't have gone this far without praying for God's help. I started getting scar tissue build-up in my vein, causing my arm to begin to tingle, so I had to quit. I had fallen short of my goal of 1000 liters!

The tingling went away, but I didn't want to risk it coming back again and causing serious problems with my arm. But, I welcome anyone who wants to break my record.

The 360 Miracle

When I was 60 years old, I did some overtime at a pharmacy in Dallas. As I was driving to work, the temperature dropped to about 29 degrees and it started snowing. I prayed that I would have a safe trip and that I wouldn't be late for work.

I was about four miles from work when I had to cross a long bridge over a river. I noticed that my car started to slide towards the curb on the right and I pumped my brake. The car pulled away from the curb, and then I started to rotate in a clock-wise direction.

As I came back to my original heading, I stopped spinning. It had seemed like everything was going in slow motion. Then I noticed a pick-up truck ahead of me, which was hardly visible in the snow. The truck had stopped and blocked two out of three lanes of traffic. I managed to go into the unoccupied lane and pass the truck.

It was just the two of us on the icy bridge, and I had faith it was because of my prayer I didn't worry about hitting the other vehicle. I was able to continue on to work without any other problems and thanked the Lord for a safe trip.

This reminds me of the fact that I have done a 180 degree turn in my life to look back on all of the blessings in my life. I have counted my blessings, named them one by one, and have been surprised what the Lord has done.

As I turn back around, I see what a real friend I have in Jesus and that He will help carry me through the rest of my life, as I trust in Him. I enjoy being friendly now, regardless of how others treat me. I'm still fighting the good fight, finishing my race, and keeping the faith. (See II Timothy 4:7)

I hope I have at least a few more laps to run in this race of life with even more miracles to come. With each day that passes, I'm one day closer to living on high. Amen, and may the Lord come soon!

APPENDIX A

Price Genealogy in America

- John Price (1584 – 1638)
  The father of:

- Joel Price (1620 – 1683)
  The father of:

- Meredith Price (1644 – 1708)
  The father of:

- Meredith Price (1670 – 1726)
  The father of:

- Bourne Price (1720 – 1758)
  The father of:

- Rev. Charles Price (1755 – 1833)
  The father of:

- Nathaniel Price (1790 – 1866)
  The father of:

- Jacob Price (1822 – 1895)
  The father of:

- James Price (1855 – 1913)
  The father of:

- Edward Price (1880 – 1974)
  The father of:

- Claude Price (1903 – 1976)
  The father of:

- Carroll Price (1929 – Present)
  The father of:

- Terry Price (1954 – Present)

APPENDIX B

Love to the World (Lyrics)

(This is my parody song from "Jeremiah Was a Bullfrog" by Hoyt Axton:)

Jesus is my Savior
He's the best friend of mine
And I believe in His Word
And all that He said
And I'll let my life so shine
And I'll let my life so shine

Love to the world
All you boys and girls
Love to the fishers from-a Galilee
Love to you and me

I'll tell you what I'll do
I'll resist all the bad
Temptations in the world
And I'll show my love to you

Love to the world
All you boys and girls
Love to the fishers from-a Galilee
Love to you and me

I'll show I love my Savior
And give Him all my laud
I'm a good soldier
And growin' bolder
I'll be a straight livin' child of my God
I'll be a straight livin' child of my God

Chorus:
Love to the world
All you boys and girls
Love to the fishers from-a Galilee
Love to you and me
Love to the world
All you boys and girls
Love to the world
Love to you and me

(Repeat chorus)

Love to the world
All you boys and girls
Love to the world
Love to you and me

APPENDIX C

We're So Glad You Came (Poem)

We're so glad you came to fellowship
In our church, today.
We're so glad you came to worship
In our church and pray.

You'll hear the good Bible preaching
In our church, today.
We hope you'll love the true teaching
In our church, we pray.

Dear Christian, Good Morning (Lyrics)

Dear Christian, good morning;
Dear Christian, good Morning.
With Jesus living in your hearts,
You're off to a wonderful start.

And so earnestly we pray,
May you have a joy that's full,
May you have a wonderful,

May you have a glorious day.
Dear Christian, good morning:
Dear Christian, good morning.
With Jesus living in our hearts,
He promised He will never part,

So, in a marvelous way
We have had a joy that's full,
We have had one wonderful,
We have had a glorious day.

APPENDIX D

How Much Faith Do I Need for Miracles to Happen?

H ebrews 11:1 says, "Now faith is the substance of things hoped for, the evidence of things not seen." (NKJV) (The words "hoped for" mean "*expected.*")

When we ask for something in faith from God, we *expect* it will happen. It is by faith we believe these things and by faith we live our lives according to what God has for us in our future.

In Matt. 17:20, it says, "So Jesus said to them 'Because of your unbelief; for assuredly, I say to you, if you have the faith as a mustard seed, you will say to this mountain 'Move from here to there' and it will move; and nothing will be impossible for you." (NKJV)

I like comparing faith to being a Red Sea crosser. When we have to make a decision in our lives that requires faith, such as crossing a "Red Sea," we have several options that we can make.

We can find other ways of crossing the sea, like looking for a boat to cross with or a nearby bridge. This is the person who doesn't look for God's help or if he does, he tries to "help God out" to get across.

Then there are those who run across because they want to get to the other side before they drown. They have little faith and are afraid that

God could change His mind as they cross over. They have a hard time accepting the fact that God is full of grace and mercy.

There are those who refuse to cross because they feel it might be a trap and that God is doing this only to drown them. These people have no faith at all and believe that God is a merciless and vengeful God.

Then there are those who walk across, that walk by faith. They keep their eyes on the Lord, Who they can see is straight ahead and watches every step they take.

Some might even sing and dance across because they have the joy of the Lord in them. These people are full of faith because they act like they aren't even aware of the possible dangers around them and know God is always watching over them and protecting them.

It really bothers me when people say that someone didn't get healed because they didn't have enough faith. If a little faith can move a mountain, then that faith should also be enough to heal someone. I know of someone who was paralyzed from a football accident from the neck down. Many people prayed for him and a lot of them had great faith. They were never able to heal him and he had an early death because of his injury. Thankfully, every Christian that dies is perfectly healed in heaven.

Jesus didn't heal everyone He met, and in fact, He had to tell some people, "Physicians, heal yourselves!" Timothy had his "often infirmities" from which he was never healed. I Timothy 5:23 says, "No longer drink only water, but use a little wine for your stomach's sake and your frequent infirmities."

Trophimus was left unhealed by Paul. II Timothy 4:20 says, "Erastmus stayed in Corinth, but Trophimus I left in Miletus sick."

Paul had a "thorn in the flesh" which he prayed for three times, to have removed and God would not take it away. II Corinthians 12:7 says, "And lest I should be exalted above measure by the abundance of the revelations, a thorn in the flesh was given to me, a messenger of Satan to buffet me, lest I be exalted above measure." I believe that God doesn't heal us sometimes because it actually helps us to grow spiritually. And by that, we learn to depend on Him more.

At the time of the Rapture, we will have new bodies that can never be injured and we will never be sick again. (I Corinthians 15:51-53) We will have this body for all eternity and this mortal life will seem to be a vapor of time in our eternal lives. (James 4:14) Our pains, emotional or physical, are only temporary.

We will all die someday, but some of us will die younger in our years than others. Each of us have our own appointment with God. (Hebrew 9:27) (Daniel 3:17-18)

APPENDIX E

Don't Mount Up Your Horse (Lyrics)

You've told me as a child when things got rough
You couldn't get along very well with your parents
You'd ride off on your horse when you had enough
'Cause the way they treated you didn't make any sense
You can't always ride away from your troubles
As a lot of your troubles will ride away with you
So, when you ride back home you face those troubles
Even worse than before and then it makes you blue

(Chorus)

Don't mount up your horse and ride away
'Cause honey I love you more each day
Oh, please I'm beggin' you to stay
And give us another chance I pray.

So. Let's stay together, our problems we will mend
Since we've been married I've only wanted you
Let's spend time together the way it had been
'Cause the love I have for you, it's so true

Let's quit looking at each other's bad faults
Let's spend more time together, you and me
Complimentin' each other gets good results
So, let's live together in sweet harmony

(Repeat chorus)

Nothing Can Compare to Eternity (Lyrics)

I know that whatever happens to me
Nothing can compare to eternity
Even though the storms may come my way
My Jesus will be with me day by day

I'll live with Him for all eternity
And I'll live with Him for all eternity
He'll get me through my pains and aches
And see me through my heartaches

As I'm on life journey's way
I'll live with Jesus some day
I'll live with Him for all eternity
And I'll live with Him for all eternity

I know that whatever happens to me
Nothing can compare to eternity
Even though we have earthquakes and lootings
No jobs much sickness and shootings

I'll live with Him for all eternity
And I'll live with Him for all eternity
He'll get me through the smoke and haze
And see me through perilous days

As I'm on life journey's way
I'll live with Jesus some day
I'll live with Him for all eternity
And I'll live with Him for all eternity

APPENDIX F

Miracles

(Puppet Play)

(Puppets: Rocky and Sandy) (Both enter)

ROCKY Sandy, what's a miracle?

SANDY A miracle is something that only God can do.

ROCKY Well, I don't understand. The other day, Mom was talking about a miracle Dad did.

SANDY Oh? What happened?

ROCKY When I came home from school, and you were at soccer practice, I saw Dad come home early from work.

SANDY (Interrupting) That's not really a miracle, Rocky.

ROCKY I know that, but it's what he did when he got home!

SANDY What happened?

ROCKY When he got home, he cleaned up the house!

SANDY It's <u>nice</u> that he did that!

ROCKY When I saw him cleaning up, I decided to clean my room, too! Then Mom came home after shopping for a few hours. When she saw that the house was clean, she dropped the bags she was carrying, raised her hands in the air and said, "It's a miracle!"

SANDY Ha, ha! That's funny!

ROCKY It really did happen, Sandy!

SANDY I mean it was funny that you cleaned up your room, too!

ROCKY What's so funny about that?

SANDY I have been praying that <u>you</u> would clean up your room!

ROCKY Ok, Ok! Do you think that Mom was praying for Dad, too?

SANDY Mom does a lot of praying, so it <u>was</u> probably and answer to her prayer.

ROCKY I haven't had many answers to my prayers. What do I have to do to help make sure God answers mine?

SANDY Psalms 66:18 says, "If I regard iniquity [or sin] in my heart, the Lord will not hear me."

ROCKY I see what you're saying! I'm gonna tell God I'm sorry for my sins and ask that He would heal Grandma's heart!

SANDY Good for you Rocky! I'm really proud of you! Does this mean that you're going to start cleaning your bedroom, too?

ROCKY Well, maybe, but don't push it! (Both exit)

The Greatest Gift (Poem)

A gift is something given
No matter how you've been;
A gift is something given
No matter if you've sinned.

Gifts aren't much of a gift
Unless it's given in love
And we have the greatest Gift
From our Father, up above.

Jesus is the greatest Gift
From the greatest Love of all;

Jesus is the greatest Gift
For our Father loves us all.

All by the Power of Jesus (Poem)

When Satan troubles us sorely,
We can claim the blood of Jesus
And resist the devil and he will flee.
When our health is felling poorly,
We know that Jesus can heal us,
By trusting in the Lord, the Almighty.
(Chorus)

All by the power of Jesus
Because he has died for us
On a hill called Calvary
And from sin, has set us free.
When our foes are all around us,
We can pray for God's protection.
Jesus can help us and make them flee.
And when they try to bring shame to us,
We can show them His affection,
Jesus can save them and make them free.
(Repeat chorus)

APPENDIX G

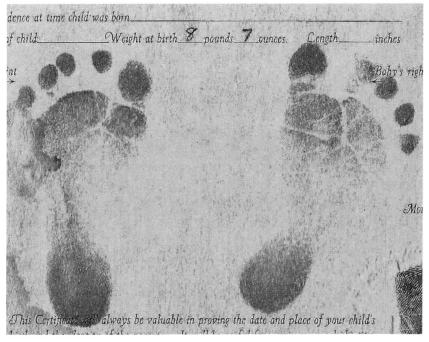

My flat feet shown on my birth certificate.

Our house in Buena Park. Tony and I are in front of
our garage. I'm holding our cat Snowball.

The twins and me in front of my house.

My first day going to kindergarten. I'm the one
holding the bag that had a rug in it.

Mom in Buena Park.

Dad, Tony, and me.

Me with Tony at Disneyland.

TJ (Teddy Joe) and me playing together.

My friend Chris in the middle wearing glasses I'm behind him to his right.

Mom in Long Beach.

Tony's first wife Nancy in Kansas City.

In my Cross Country uniform.

Tony with his daughters Kristi and Melissa

Cindy and me a few months after we were married.

At my first duty station, Ft. Benning.

Training on the Big Island of Hawaii with Moana Kea behind me.

Donald (Donny) and Debra (Debi) in Fayetteville, N.C.

Jeremy, me and Jonathan (Jon) in Fayetteville, N.C.

TJ, Tracy and Patrick

The last picture I have of TJ.

Ethan, Jeremy, Caleb and Jonathan (Ethan and Caleb are Debra's sons) Caleb is the one who inspired me to write this book.

Marge and Dad on his 85th birthday. Marge is Dad's second wife.

Cindy and me in Cabo, San Lucas, Mexico

Me as the world record holder.

About the Author

I had many memories of my childhood that I kept. I often thought about writing a diary about all of the interesting things that happened in my life. I now have the time to write a memoir with a theme. I decided to write about the miracles that happened in my life and those close to me.

I was in the army and worked security for a good part of my life. During those times, my wife and I had some very unusual things happen to us. God gave me a vision that lead to wonderful miracles which drew me closer to the Lord and also changed the life of others.

I recently broke a world record while helping others with their health. Today, I still work in the security field and hold a Private Investigator's license. I hope that by telling about these miracles throughout my life, they would be